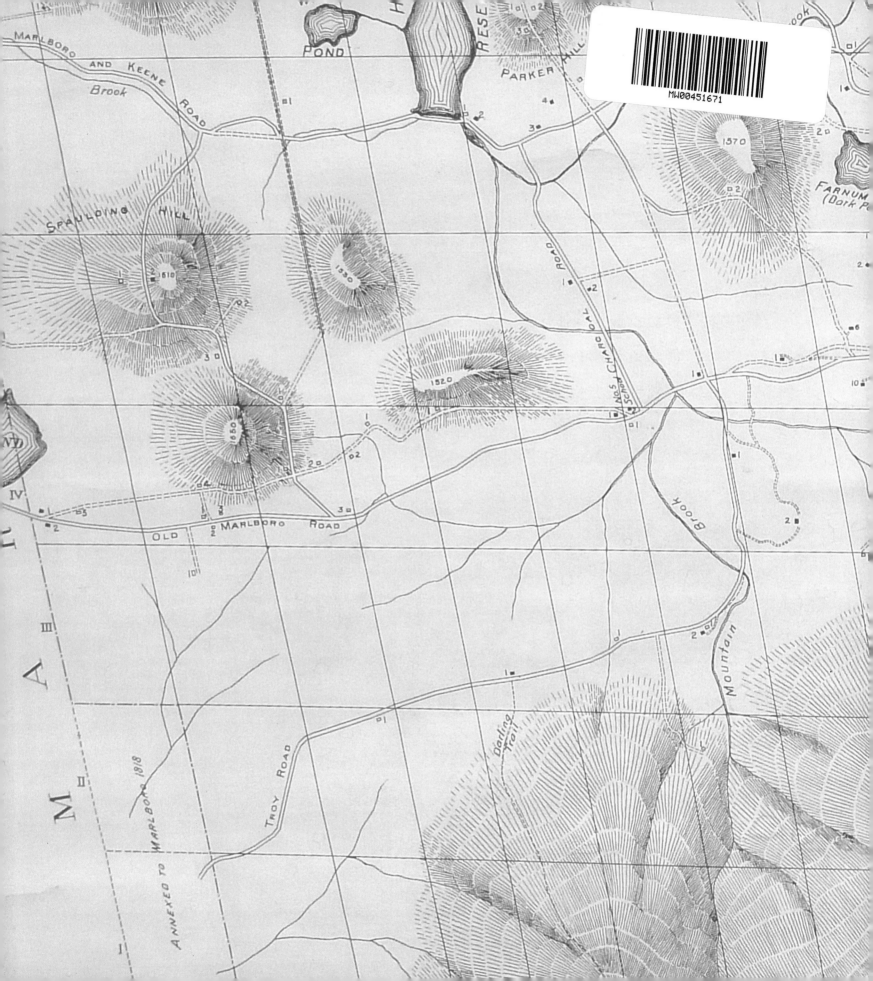

When we build let us think we build forever. Let it not be for present delight nor for present use alone. Let it be such work that our descendants will thank us for, and let us think, as we lay stone upon stone, that a time is to come when these stones will be held sacred because our hands have touched them, and that men will say, as they look upon the labor and wrought substance of them, 'See! This our fathers did for us.'

John Ruskin (1819 - 1900)

Stonlea

A Peabody & Stearns Summer House
in the Monadnock Region of New Hampshire

Stonlea

A Timeworn, Gilded Age Survivor Transformed

Peter W. Clement
Victoria Chave Clement

2014

BAUHAN PUBLISHING
PETERBOROUGH, NEW HAMPSHIRE

ISBN: 978-0-87233-179-2

Library of Congress Cataloging-in-Publication Data

Clement, Peter W., 1946-
  Stonlea : a timeworn gilded age survivor transformed / Peter W. Clement & Victoria Chave Clement.
    pages cm
  "A Peabody & Stearns summer house in the Monadnock region of New Hampshire. The story of a time-worn Gilded Age survivor transformed into a handsome and sustainable year round, family house."
  Includes bibliographical references and index.
  ISBN 978-0-87233-179-2 (alk. paper)
  1. Stonlea (Dublin, N.H.) 2. Catlin, Daniel, 1837-1916--Homes and haunts--New Hampshire--Dublin. 3. Peabody & Stearns (Boston, Mass.) 4. Architecture, Domestic--Conservation and restoration--New Hampshire--Dublin. 5. Vacation homes--Conservation and restoration--New Hampshire--Dublin. 6. Dublin (N.H.)--Buildings, structures, etc. I. Clement, Victoria Chave, 1949- II. Title.
  NA737.P6C59 2014
  728.809742'9--dc23

                    2014016675

Published for Polly W. Guth by Bauhan Publishing, LLC
Text by Peter W. Clement
Book design by Victoria Chave Clement – Chave Design, Madison, Connecticut
Typeset in Jan Tschichold's Sabon, Erik Spiekermann's FF Meta, and Matthew Carter's Skia
Printed by GHP Media, West Haven, Connecticut

Front endpaper: Map of Dublin, New Hampshire from the survey by Thomas Fisk, 1853 (with additions and corrections by Samuel Wadsworth, 1906), courtesy of the Dublin Historical Society
Back endpaper: Floor plans of Stonlea by Peter W. Clement, adapted from Peabody & Stearns and Daniel V. Scully
Cover watercolor from Peabody & Stearns collection at the Boston Public Library, Fine Arts Department
Front cover inset photograph and back cover photograph by Peter W. Clement

PO BOX 117 PETERBOROUGH NEW HAMPSHIRE 03458
603-567-4430
WWW.BAUHANPUBLISHING.COM

Distributed by University Press of New England
Lebanon, New Hampshire
WWW.UPNE.ORG

I am dedicating this book to Hugh Hardy.

Without his encouragement, enthusiasm,
special talents and exemplary courage,
this project would never have happened.

Polly Guth

Of all the lives the house has enjoyed, I do believe it is now at its best, adapting to the informal way we all now live.

Hugh Hardy

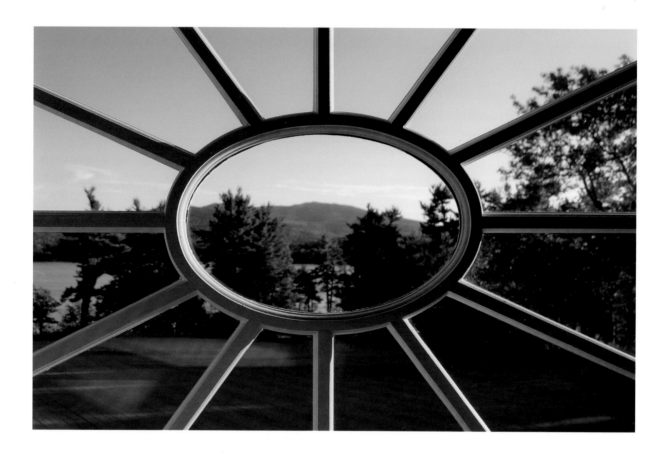

Dear Reader,

You have stumbled upon a rare story … or perhaps a well-known one. The adventures of repairing and renovating a house, in this case a large one: a nineteenth-century summer house called Stonlea, in New Hampshire.

The difference between a rare and well-known story, in this case, is the scale of the project. The house is quite large, and the finishes and details of the original house are beautiful. But the journey that we owners of old houses take will be a familiar one: the questions of what to repair? how to do it? where to find the craftsmen? how much of an investment in energy savings to make?

This book tells the story of taking a Gilded Age grande dame of a summer house, designed in 1890 by Boston architects Peabody & Stearns, and making it into a comfortable, year-round family house.

Why did I preserve and restore this large ark of a house? I think that it is a matter of *stewardship*. That is, caring for a house that was noteworthy when it was built, in 1891, and is noteworthy again, 120 years later. And for more reasons than just having fresh paint and a new roof: I wanted to account for the demands of climate change.

There is also the question of *continuity*. The original owner and I had similar goals: We wanted a country house for family and friends to visit, in a pristine highland environment. The catalyst for me was the birth nearby of my GREAT-granddaughter … think of it! Four generations.

There's much to tell you. The book is about how the house was lived in when it was designed, and how the design has been altered over time, to fit each generation's "modern-day" use. Find what's interesting to you. You don't have to read about everything. We hope we won't frighten you away. The renovation process is demanding in many ways, but it is so satisfying once it's done.

Yours sincerely,

Polly

July 9, 2012

Dear Polly:

How good it was for us to be with you at Stonlea recently. No longer do I have to imagine what it's like for you to be there: I have memorable proof. As a result, I began to think how it all began, with my trip to Dublin, and the general idea that you could simplify travel logistics and create a single, accessible place for receiving family and friends, with daughter, granddaughter & great-granddaughter, right next door. Now it is all true.

Obviously, it is a great joy for all your friends to see you there, as well as for the family. It will become an even more valuable experience with many gathered together.

I am impressed that every room already seems lived-in, rather than showy-new, and delight in rediscovering old furniture friends from Corning. It amuses me that having banished the formal dining room, it turns out you can eat anywhere, depending on the number of people: that each different place can match the occasion, indoors or out, grand or intimate. You have the gift of making people feel welcome in any setting, so the variety of rooms encourages that exploration.

I do like the openness of the first floor and vistas between the different rooms. You can enjoy this without having to wander through them. It's also fun to see, in addition to the lake and mountain vistas, how when sitting in the Lake Room there are also views to the far end of the kitchen, and out the front door. Somehow it all makes that room seem more cozy, set inside its mahogany enclosure.

The landscape does suit the house: it is integrated with the land. And the kitchen terrace greatly enhances the outdoor life of the place. I especially like contrasts between groomed and wild expanses of lawn, giving definition to different vistas, and hints of far off places to explore.

Of all the lives the house has enjoyed, I do believe it is now at its best, adapting to the informal way we all now live. Since we have become our own servants, and the formal separations of labor and turf have happily been eroded, it seems better to enjoy a more open interior rather than a set of formal divisions between rooms. I was also pleased to see that people look good in those places, they really do, and that clearly contributes to a general feeling of well-being.

Thank you for all this. Makes me proud.

Best Wishes,

Hugh

H³ HARDY COLLABORATION ARCHITECTURE LLC
902 Broadway New York New York 10010 Tel 212 677 6030 Fax 212 979 0535 www.h3hc.com

contents

1891

2011

stewardship & preservation
caring for the future

HOW OLD was your house when you were born?
How long will it survive after you have moved on? We're
all stewards of the built environment, as we're stewards
of our children. The generational hand-offs of we humans
are short compared to the lifespan of a well-built house.
And we're stewards of the natural environment. These
two concerns came together pointedly when it was time
to plan the renovation of this house.

Polly's herculean effort to restore Stonlea to health and modern
use is based on her strong sense of stewardship. Members of her family
continue to own a substantial house in Orford, New Hampshire, built by
an ancestor in 1814.

Particularly in this age of rapid turnover—of products, of houses,
of neighborhoods, and of attention spans—it seemed important to her to
preserve the well-wrought work of this house. It had been carefully sited,
carefully laid out, and well built. It represents a period of robust growth
in American history, the fruit of the industrial revolution. At the same
time the house is not a palace: It has fewer rooms than you might expect,
but they are generously proportioned. It is difficult to find a house of this
period with this combination of scale and livability.

A new, very large-scale summer house, built with punch, can cost
eight figures. How many weather-worn houses, with distinguished design
lineage, are still awaiting their salvation? How much more of a house do
you get, when craftsmen of a century ago have carved their lost art into it?

Stonlea in 1893, shortly after it was finished

introduction

STONLEA is a large *Colonial Revival** style
summer house in New England, a vivid example of
nineteenth-century resort architecture. It was completed
in 1891 by a family from St. Louis, seeking to escape the
withering summers on the Mississippi River. The house
was designed by the well known Boston architecture firm
of Peabody & Stearns, who were very busy in the late
nineteenth century, designing country houses that helped
shape the new face of resort architecture in the northeast.

It was built to accommodate a family of five and their domestic
help, as well as long-term guests, and it therefore met the requirements
of the present owner, who wanted to house visiting family members and
make the house a gathering place for four generations.

The house is sited overlooking Dublin Lake, originally called
Monadnock Lake, with picturesque Mount Monadnock beyond. The
original property included the house, a barn, a cottage, and a large carriage house/garage, on approximately one hundred acres of ancient farmland. By 2009 the house's outbuildings had been sold to Polly's daughter,
so the latest purchase reassembled a large piece of the original puzzle.

The house had survived over one hundred years of New England
weather and hard summer living fairly well, but had begun to suffer from
"*deferred maintenance*," a circumstance familiar to all homeowners. The
task of bringing the house back to its original luster was a formidable
one. In addition, the owner wanted to bring to bear the latest technology
to reduce its impact on the environment: She wanted a "green" house, or
more specifically a "*net-zero*" house, referring to the balancing of energy
consumed and energy produced on-site.

* *Words shown in italics refer to definitions in the Glossary.*

When the size of the house is considered, at 12,000 square feet, the project becomes complicated, and interesting.

A team of architects and engineering consultants was assembled to plan this complex project. This book will parse the numerous and various areas of concern, and describe this large project in a way that would inform any similar undertaking, regardless of size.

The book will address the renovation of the *fabric* of the building, the various energy-conserving strategies, and the mechanical systems. It will also address the whys and wherefores of the design of the house, to bring the house designed for a non-electrified, full-service staff into the more participatory family life of today.

A mural in the Dublin library combining features from several New Hampshire towns. The mountain dominates.

the setting
farmsteads to country retreats

DHS

DUBLIN, New Hampshire, was founded in 1752, and was the home of farmsteads until the mid-nineteenth century. As farming in the area became less productive, a succession of families from the city, Boston primarily, began to change the character of the place. The first new summer settlers were taking advantage of post-Civil War prosperity that allowed for new levels of discretionary income and, as importantly, discretionary time. The expanding railroads also facilitated travel to remote areas.

In seeking a summer retreat, one often looks for natural advantages in the setting. Dublin had the lake, the highland climate (in this case always referred to as salubrious), the woodland trails, the open and scenic farmland, and the mountain, which offered healthful exercise as well as a striking backdrop to the lake. The town's higher altitude (1,440 feet above sea level) meant that the weather was cooler and drier than its lowland and seaside counterparts.

The railroads were almost an embarrassment of riches. Mark Twain, a renter for two seasons, in 1905 and 1906, was reputed to say that to get there from Hartford, he changed trains as often as he thought about it.

The mountain and lake from the northeast

Carriage and pony-cart rides were a popular form of entertainment; the latter, especially, for unescorted children.

Early transportation, with the lake and the mountain beyond. The photographer is counting on his horses to stay put.

Those who have "discovered" a place, if they are enthusiastic about promoting their idyll, set off a daisy-chain of references to friends and relations: House-guests become entranced with the place, and come back as hotel guest, renter, home-owner, and in turn invite their friends. The new seasonal settlers in this case were artists and intellectuals, along with their patrons, who were looking for simplicity and beauty. They formed an initial colony on the south side of the lake, known as the Latin Quarter, primarily set in the woods.

Diminutive cottages in the trees were followed by small *Shingle Style* houses, with colorful names like Banjo Cottage, Owl's Nest, and The Thistles, a tradition to this day. These two building types blended well with their woodland settings, and retreat and contemplation were the order of the day.

With the arrival of the *Gilded Age*, another wave of summer folk arrived, with unheard-of riches to spend. Their houses were built bigger and bolder. They were larger Shingle Style and *Queen Anne* houses, and later more classically proportioned houses. They sat out in the middle of former farm fields, for the views, and for all to see. Stonlea was among these later arrivals.

Daniel Catlin, a prosperous tobacco producer, was visiting friends from St. Louis in the summer of 1889. George Eliot Leighton had built a striking Shingle Style house in 1888. It was an early entrant in the emergence of the larger house and their extended "estates," a word that had not been applied to earlier houses in the area. Catlin liked what he saw, and his host suggested that the family buy the nearby farm on the north side of the lake. They did so that same August, and immediately hired the same architects as their host, the prolific Boston designers Peabody & Stearns, who conveniently had an office in St. Louis. The old farmhouse was removed, and the new house was under construction through the summer of 1890, while the new owners rented a house nearby, in anticipation (and probably for better supervision) of the construction.

What was the norm for a sizeable summer house in 1890? What were the models for a family wishing to make a place for their family and friends to gather? A carriage tour of the area would reveal a variety of summer cottage styles.

the neighborhood
the country house comes of age

MORSE/CLARK HOUSE –1822

Nineteenth-century houses become summer retreats. This house was built by Thaddeus Morse, in the Federal style. It was later purchased by Grenville Clark as a summer house, and remains in his family.

GREENE COTTAGE –1872

An example of an early summer settler's house. It has an unselfconscious design, a "vernacular" look, designed for ease of living. The builder of this cottage was an early advocate of Dublin as a summer retreat for artists and poets.

OWL'S NEST – 1885

Typical of the next generation of houses in Dublin is Owl's Nest, one of three houses built for summer rental between 1884 and 1886. Like many of the smaller houses of this time, it was designed in the Shingle Style, and is situated in the trees, not far from the lake. Their pheasant-like colorings make them difficult to see among the trees, which was very much the point.

MONADNOCK FARMS – Peabody & Stearns -1888

DPL: HDA

This is the house that inspired the Catlins. It was among the first large houses in the town that had seen its wooded and farm lands converted to summer use. Several large farms were purchased and cleared for construction of houses that, like this one, demand your attention and invite your admiration.

This house shares a make-up similar to Stonlea; it has three distinct blocks: a dormered staff wing to the south (left), a prominent central block, featuring a tower with aerial loggia, and a bold north wing with surrounding piazza. The simplicity of the north wing, with its large, equal-sized windows, and deep, dark porch openings, makes it a powerful beast in its pastoral setting. The two small eyebrow windows in the roof, while trying not to detract from the mass, give the look of a sleepy serpent.

*Stonlea from the south, shortly after it was completed in 1891.
The front gable and the predominate use of clapboards signal a
Colonial Revival house that has a distinctive Shingle Style east wing.
Note the absence of trees: This was until only recently farmland.*

DPL: HDA

*View from Stonlea's curved balcony towards
Mount Monadnock and Dublin Lake. The
pony cart is on the original road in front of
the house. A stone path leads to the formal
front door of the house.*

DHS

introducing the house
the grand summer cottage arrives

STONLEA is more formal than its nearby kinsman, Monadnock Farms: It is composed mostly of Colonial Revival design features, with a distinctly Shingle Style staff wing to the east. It features nearly all of the characteristics of a Colonial Revival house: wrap-around *piazza*, highly articulated *portico* with two-story columns, oval window, porch rails with finials, *pilasters* at the front porch, oval accent windows (at the rear), painted *clapboard* siding, and white accents.

The *façade* has four parts: The Living/Master Bedroom wing, on the left (west), with its wrap-around Piazza, bay window, and highly detailed windows and dormers; the central Hall section, with its dominant columns, lacy porch rails, and decorated gable end; the Dining Room/Guest Room block, with its broad, simpler details; and the shingled and *gambrel-roofed* kitchen/staff wing to the east. Each block is "bent" back from the next, forming an elliptical plan that gives views of the lake and mountain to the south. The result is a comfortable fit with its prominent, sloping site.

The Piazza wrapped around the *Parlor* from the front porch, ending at an overlook called a *Belvedere*, with its rounded roof. The three equal dormers on the east wing are clearly visible here. The wing has a gambrel roof, whose second pitch was also the wall of the rooms. The wing is covered in shingles on the second floor, and clapboards on the first floor.

South

SOUTH ELEVATION

P&S/BPL/PWC

The South Elevation, drawn by Peabody & Stearns. The doorway to the Hall, and doors to the bedrooms upstairs, are off-center due to the fanning geometry of the plan. Note oval window.

North

NORTH ELEVATION

P&S/BPL/PWC

The North Elevation. The main entrance was under the large Palladian window. The roofs take some twists and turns to accommodate the main staircase. The rendering shows corrections to the first floor roof, left of the big window; the design appears to have been in flux when this rendering was made. This is endemic to the practice of architecture, an example of designers' perpetual optimism.

East

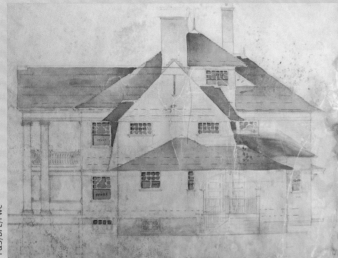

P&S/BPL/PWC

The East Elevation. This view shows the tall porch columns from the side. The arch pencilled under the low roof remains, part of the Pea-Shelling Porch. They were still working on those roofs at the stairs, to the right.

West

WEST ELEVATION

P&S/BPL/PWC

The West Elevation. The size of the Piazza is evident here. The fan-shaped roof to the left was the Belvedere. The India ink spill suggests that this was a draft rendering; certainly it was after the spill.

Views of the surrounding country, c. 1910. Old farmland was beginning to grow over with second-growth trees, and the more substantial farmhouses were becoming summer houses.

Stonlea, c. 1898, after the Billiard Room and Office were added to the west, but before the east wing was modified in 1903

Cutting ice on Dublin Lake, with Stonlea in the distance.

The south side of Stonlea, 1891

Stonlea, 1891

This photograph shows the Porte-Cochère, built in 1898 and removed in the 1916 renovations.

Main drive coming off the old Keene road

The house here has grown hoary with plantings, around and on the building. The steps to the left were part of a garden enclosure in front of the house, that was gone by 2009.

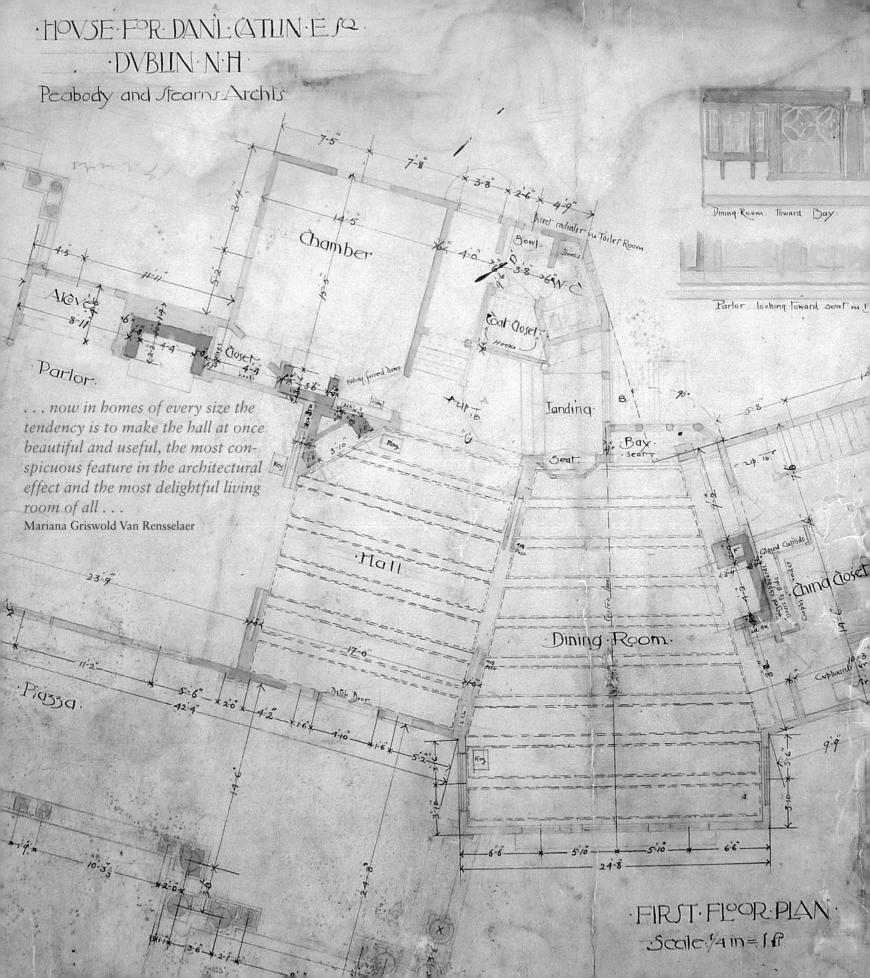

HOVSE FOR DANL CATLIN ESQ
DVBLIN N H
Peabody and Stearns Archts

Chamber

Alcove

Parlor.

. . . *now in homes of every size the tendency is to make the hall at once beautiful and useful, the most conspicuous feature in the architectural effect and the most delightful living room of all* . . .
Mariana Griswold Van Rensselaer

Closet

Bowl
W C
Coat Closet

Landing

Bay
Seat.

.Hall

Dining Room. toward Bay

Parlor looking toward seat in

Glazed Cupbds
China Closet

Piazza.

Dutch Door.

Dining Room.

Cupboards

FIRST FLOOR PLAN.
Scale ¼ in = 1 ft

inside the house
a walking tour

STONLEA was designed in a style called Colonial Revival, with elements of the Shingle Style. Emerging out of a progression of American house design in the 1860s and 1870s, the Shingle Style consisted of larger, freely flowing volumes of space, which broke up the "center-hall" layout of so many colonial houses. The house would then be wrapped in a uniform, cedar-shingled surface, walls and roof, often creating a formidable presence.

The Colonial Revival style included more articulation: varieties of window *muntin* patterns; overhanging eaves with dentils; more or less ornate columns; siding that included clapboards, shingles, and pilasters; diamond patterns in the shingles; *pedimented* gables; and porches or a piazza that ran across much of the façade. Most of these elements can be found in the original Stonlea.

The original drawings by Peabody & Stearns appear to be "presentation drawings," with fine watercolor washes, for the client to see how the design would look. However, the floor plans show dimensions, for the contractor's use in the actual construction process, so they are a charming hybrid.

1891 – First Floor Plan, Peabody & Stearns Drawings. The drawings were damaged in a fire, not by flames, but by heat that melted a bitumen lining behind the drawings. The drawings are now stabilized and preserved in the Boston Public Library, Fine Arts Collection.

They are handsomely and meticulously drawn, and rendered with a color wash on both the elevations (façades), and the floor plans. The exterior walls are rendered as yellow, and the roof as red. Early black-and-white photographs show the house with lighter corner *frieze-boards*, columns, and window trim, and the clapboards of the main block of the house as slightly darker; probably yellow.

First Floor

For formal visits, you arrived at the house on the lake side, from an old track that remained from the original farm (see photo on page 26). You entered the house up a stone walk to broad stone steps at the Front Porch. This outdoor room was surrounded by columns, and was the most formal outdoor space. It connected to the Piazza, on the left, known as the "summer porches" to the family. They were broad, deep spaces where much of the day's activities took place: One could sit in the shade, take in the summer breezes, avoid the rain, and look out at the lake to the south. It was a place where the family could be found at any time of the

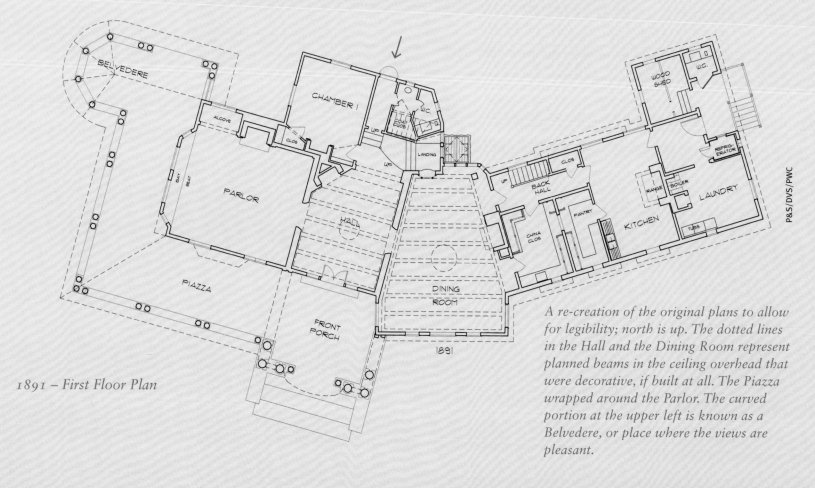

1891 – First Floor Plan

A re-creation of the original plans to allow for legibility; north is up. The dotted lines in the Hall and the Dining Room represent planned beams in the ceiling overhead that were decorative, if built at all. The Piazza wrapped around the Parlor. The curved portion at the upper left is known as a Belvedere, or place where the views are pleasant.

day, and where visitors were entertained informally. It was a very generous fourteen-and-a-half-feet deep, and wrapped around the Parlor on the south and west sides. The porches culminated, at the northwest corner of the house, in a Belvedere, or place of pleasant views.

Entering the Hall, you faced a door that led to a rear entrance, with W.C. and Coat Closet. At the right was a compact but gracious staircase, and to the left was a room with a fireplace, which was designated a "Chamber" in the drawings. While this label was usually reserved for bedrooms, this room seems more likely to have been an office for conducting the business of the house. This room was later redesigned as an entry foyer when a breezeway was formed to connect the Hall to the new Billiard Room at the west. The office use then transferred, not surprisingly, to the "Office."

To the left (east) of the Hall is the large Parlor, or living room. The west wall formed a long bay, with window seat. Depending on the weather, and the formality of the occasion, this room alternated with the Hall and the Piazza. From the Hall, the Dining Room is to the right. A chandelier indicated that the dining table was placed in the middle of the room, opposite the fireplace. Over time the table migrated towards the south-facing windows, where it sits today.

Certainly no really comfortable country home can exist in our land without a piazza.
Mariana Griswold Van Rensselaer

A view of a piazza in a house of the same period in Lenox, Massachusetts, with similar view of lake and hills.

The service wing is to the east, made up of four separate rooms connected by pass-throughs, and a service corridor. From the Dining Room eastward the rooms are labeled China Closet, Pantry, Kitchen, and Laundry. In the Kitchen was a seven-and-a-half-foot-long soapstone sink and a wood-burning, cast-iron "Range" under a large iron hood that hung from a very big brick chimney. Behind, and sharing the chimney, was the Laundry, with a wood-fired hot water heater, irons heater, and large tubs.

The "Refrigerator," or literally icebox, was a small insulated room, with a thick door and a sizeable brass latch. It was accessed by the staff from inside the house, while the ice man could supply his blocks of ice (harvested from the lake in the winter) through a small access door, placed high in the exterior wall of the porch: placed high, since cold air falls. For some time, the icebox has functioned as a wine cellar.

A firewood storage room, at the northeast corner of the house, supplied the constant demand of the Range and the Laundry, in addition to the fireplaces. It could be restocked through an outside access door. A covered open porch, facing east, was added in 1903.

Icebox door from the Pea-Shelling Porch

The kitchen from The Mark Twain House & Museum, in Hartford, Connecticut. Stonlea's kitchen was probably not too different from this one. The work table was the focus of most of the work in the kitchen.

Icebox door from the kitchen

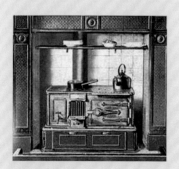

Period range

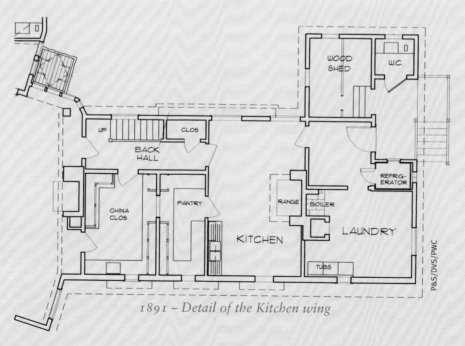

1891 – Detail of the Kitchen wing

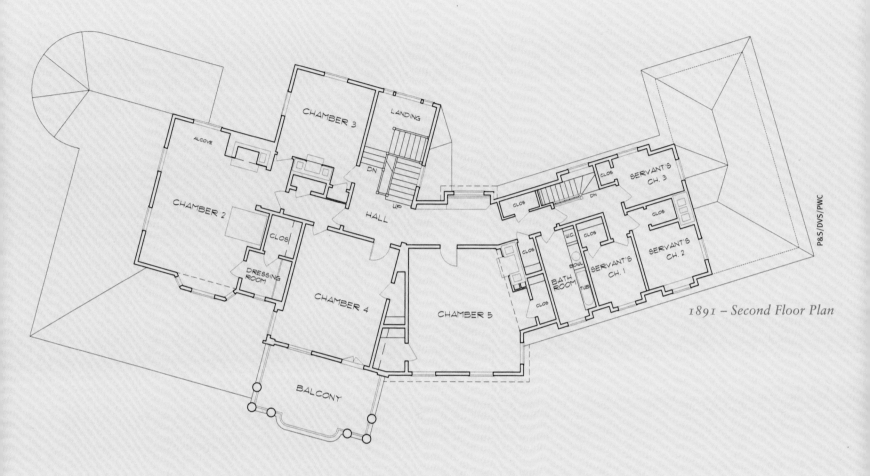

P&S/DVS/PWC

1891 – Second Floor Plan

Second Floor

The house had six family bedrooms, noted on the drawings as "Chambers" (to be referred to as bedrooms here), most with fireplaces. The family had a daughter (fifteen) and two sons (fourteen and thirteen).

The west bedroom (#2), over the living room, was the master bedroom: It had a niche (with a bed lightly sketched in on the drawings), and was the only room with closet space and dressing room built in. It opened onto two of the other bedrooms, north and south, without one having to enter the upstairs hall. This arrangement allowed for a boudoir, or for varied spousal sleeping arrangements.

The south bedroom (#4), is a large guest room, opening onto the Balcony, a porch covered by the central roof gable. It was supported by columns running at the corners through to the roof. An elaborately turned and curved balcony railing was a feature of the original façade.

The east bedroom (#5) was another large guest room. Beyond the east bedroom was the Bath Room, the only such room in the house—literally a bathing room—between the family and staff quarters. It contained a W.C. or toilet, a "Bowl" or sink, and a seven-foot-long, narrow Tub. Chamber pots must have eased the pressure on this room; bathing times were no doubt strictly regulated. The staff probably made do with wash basins in their rooms.

Beyond the Bath Room was a door in the hall that separated the family spaces from the staff. Beyond were three servants' rooms, probably housing two staff members each. This area was altered several times before the 2011 work was done. To the right of the chimney outside the east servant's room is the roof of the Laundry, Wood Room, and W.C. below. This roof was absorbed into the 1903 expansion of both the first and second floors. The three small dormers, visible in the exterior photos, were represented in this plan by the bays at the Bath Room and servants' rooms #1 and #2.

1891 – Second Floor Plan – Staff Wing
Plan reconstructed due to damaged originals.

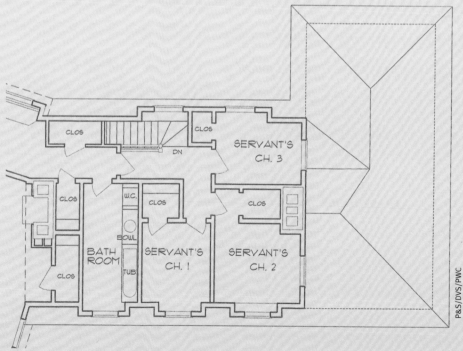

Third Floor

Up under the roof of the large, west gable of the house was the "Boy's Room," a large playroom with a fireplace and three dormers with views of the lake and fields behind the house. It is likely that the two boys moved up to the bedroom (#6) immediately, since they were old enough to be on their own. A Store Room, in the porch gable on the original plans, became a bathroom when the gable was pushed back in 1916, and remains so. It features a new oval window, similar to the original, replacing a *Palladian* window that was introduced in the interim. The three dormers of the service wing are seen on the right of the plan.

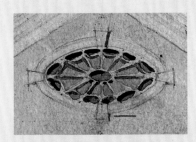

Original Peabody & Stearns rendering of the oval window on third floor

Boy's Room dormer as it looks today

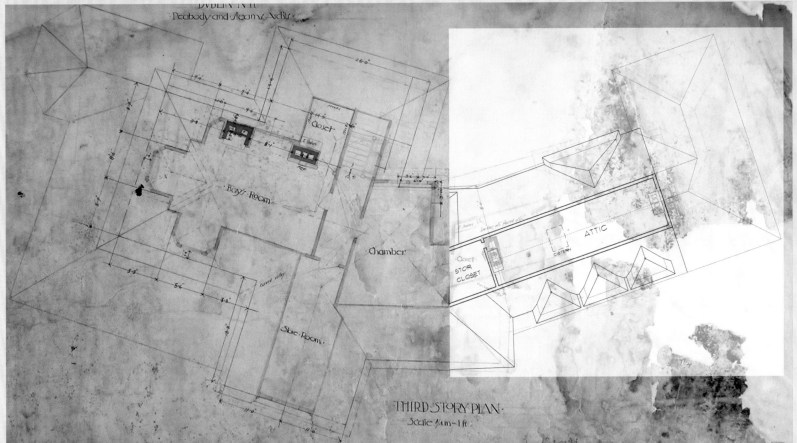

1891 – Third Floor Plan with reconstructed overlay due to damaged originals

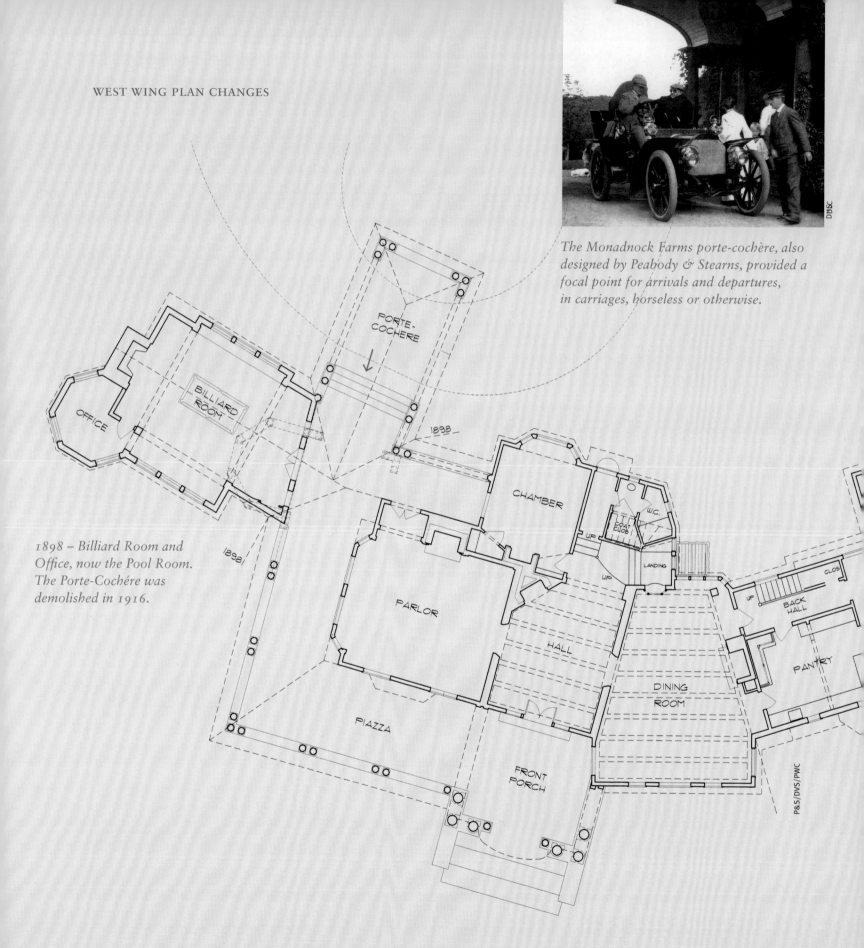

The Monadnock Farms porte-cochère, also designed by Peabody & Stearns, provided a focal point for arrivals and departures, in carriages, horseless or otherwise.

1898 – Billiard Room and Office, now the Pool Room. The Porte-Cochére was demolished in 1916.

PORTE-COCHERE

OFFICE

BILLIARD ROOM

1898

1898

CHAMBER

W.C.

COAT CLOS

LANDING

UP

UP

UP

PARLOR

HALL

BACK HALL

CLOS

PANTRY

DINING ROOM

PIAZZA

FRONT PORCH

P&S/DV5/PWC

renovations
changes over time

BEGINNING IN 1898, large additions and renovations were made. At the west, where the Belvedere was situated, these included the Billiard Room, sometimes referred to as the Smoking Room, and a small, octagonal room off of it called the Office. The Billiard Room had large triple windows overlooking the lake to the south, and fields to the north. There was a fireplace at the west end, that had a Delft tile surround, and exposed trusses overhead that were painted with elaborate armorial patterns. The composition of the two new rooms, and the elaborate chimney, was very picturesque. It canted away from the lake, in a continuation of the long arc of the plan.

The downstairs room acquired a bay window and may have taken on another use. A breezeway became the new entry point, under a new *Porte-Cochère*, with a doorway into the Parlor.

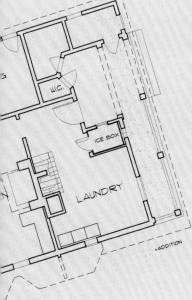

Kitchen wing with servants rooms on second floor

DPL: HDA

DLC

The owner's son at the Porte-Cochère, c.1900. At the horse's head are the windows to the Billiard Room, with their distinctive muntin layout. The steps under the Porte-Cochère led to the new breezeway, visible through the columns.

Electricity was introduced to Dublin around 1899. Sometime soon afterwards the house was retrofitted with wiring, which would have required extensive intrusion into the interior finishes. Wiring each room for a chandelier simplified, somewhat, the wiring and lighting task. (In 2008 there were ceiling junction boxes for twenty-two chandeliers.) Plumbing installations, even more intrusive, and very welcome, were probably done at the same time.

EAST WING PLAN CHANGES

Peabody & Stearns designed substantial changes to the staff wing. In this work the first floor was extended four-and-a-half feet east, and has become known as the Pea-Shelling Porch, in honor of its role as relaxation point for the cooking staff, who nonetheless continued to prepare for dinner. The columns supporting the floor above the porch are handsomely curved at their tops.

The major change to the house then was the enlargement of the second-floor staff wing which was extended about twenty feet east past the Kitchen/Laundry chimney, and north. Two of the three small dormers were removed and the third, west dormer, was incorporated into the new design. The new large dormers reflected the expanded space inside. The resulting shingled façade exists today.

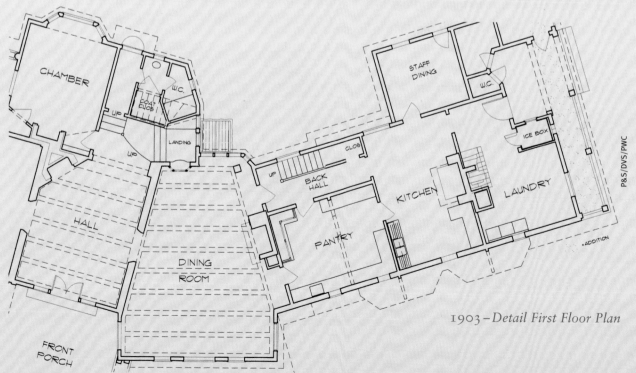

1903 – Detail First Floor Plan

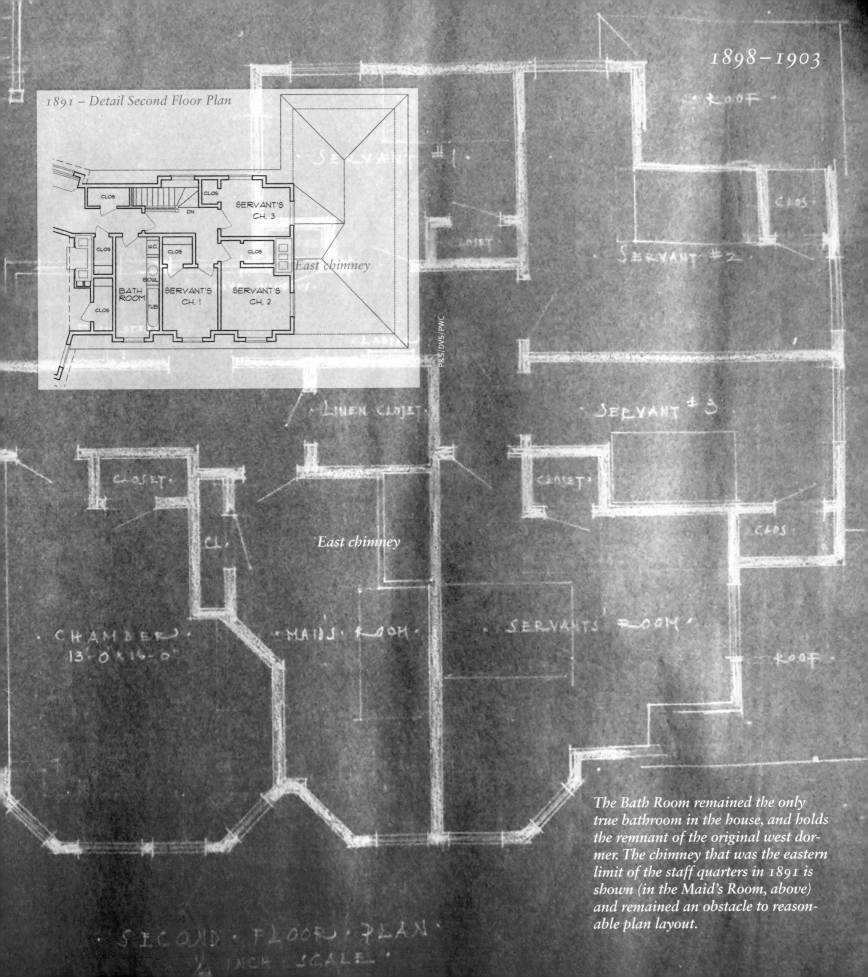

ROOF

SERVANT #1

CLOS·

CLOSET

SERVANT #2·

SERVANT #3

CLOSET·

CLOS·

1891 – Detail Second Floor Plan

CLOS

CLOS

SERVANT'S
CH. 3

DN

W.C.

CLOS

CLOS

East chimney

CLOS

BATH
ROOM

BOWL

SERVANT'S
CH. 1

SERVANT'S
CH. 2

TUB

P&S/DVS/PWC

·LINEN·CLOSET·

·CLOSET·

East chimney

CL·

·CHAMBER·
13'-0"×16'-0"

·MAID'S·ROOM·

·SERVANTS'·ROOM·

·ROOF·

The Bath Room remained the only
true bathroom in the house, and holds
the remnant of the original west dormer. The chimney that was the eastern
limit of the staff quarters in 1891 is
shown (in the Maid's Room, above)
and remained an obstacle to reason-
able plan layout.

·SECOND·FLOOR·PLAN·
¼ INCH SCALE·

The original east wing with its three small dormers. The Kitchen wing had reduced views of the lake, and no doors to the south.

1891 – Partial South Elevation

A detail photograph of the east wing in 1893, showing the original delicate dormers, with their copper cap pieces, against the gambrel roof. The first floor was clad in clapboards, but the Shingle Style was making a modest appearance.

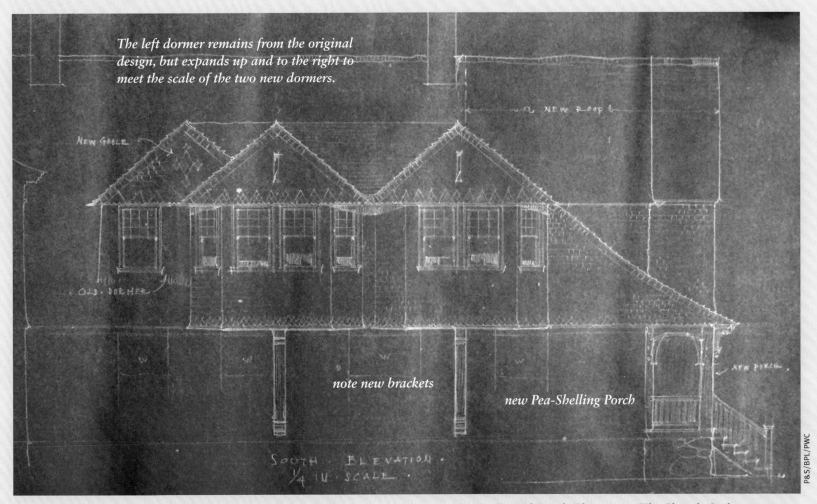

The left dormer remains from the original design, but expands up and to the right to meet the scale of the two new dormers.

note new brackets

new Pea-Shelling Porch

1903 – Partial South Elevation—The Shingle Style returns

2008 – The two big dormers' roofs funneled rainwater directly over the later kitchen door. An attempt was made to guide the water away, obscuring the single buttresses under each dormer. The gutters appeared to be saluting, ambidextrously.

2011 – With new doors located under the bays' new twin brackets, rainwater now pours into a catch basin in the terrace, avoiding any guttering at all.

1891 – East Elevation. Half of the staff wing is one story. This elevation shows the gambrel roof which will soon be absorbed into the 1903 changes.

2009 – East Elevation

1903 – East Elevation

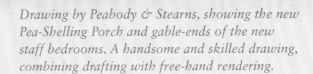

P&S/BPL/PWC

Drawing by Peabody & Stearns, showing the new Pea-Shelling Porch and gable-ends of the new staff bedrooms. A handsome and skilled drawing, combining drafting with free-hand rendering.

2011 – East Elevation with new garage to the north

2008 – An aerial view from the north, highlighting the complex roof and dormers.

small gable

P&S/BPL/PWC

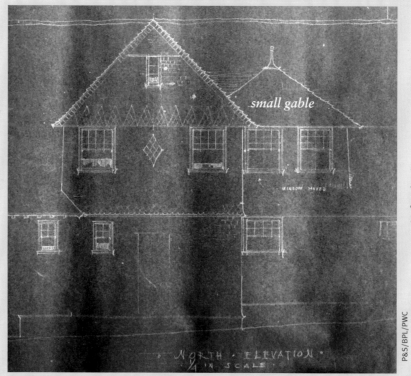

small gable

1903 – Partial North elevation. The smaller gable was part of the 1891 construction. It was somewhat crowded by the new gable, built in the expansion of the wing.

P&S/BPL/PWC

2008–Partial North elevation

DVS

The north side of the staff wing, before the renovations began. The bigger 1903 gable lacks the canted eaves, and finesse, of its predecessor. The stone wall separated the public arrival point from the back-of-the-house: laundry lines, dog run, etc.

small gable

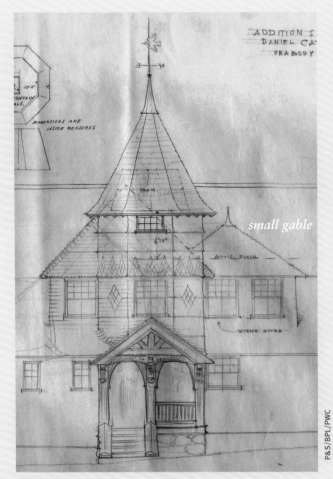

P&S/BPL/PWC

A design for a proposed water tower addition, and new rear entrance for the north side, that was never executed. You can see the architects sketching different dormer alternatives: small, medium, large. Peabody & Stearns demonstrate here their facility with picturesque designs. Compare to the more classical south elevation.

small gable

2011–Partial North elevation, with garage to the left

Sometime after the summer of 1916, following the death of Daniel Catlin, the house was radically altered. Probably as a matter of changing tastes, the front porch with its monumental columns, delicate railings, and dominant pediment, was removed. A new gable was built back at the front plane of the Hall/Guest Room portion of the building, and the summer porches were removed. A third-floor bathroom was made in the storage area under the reduced gable, with a new Palladian window.

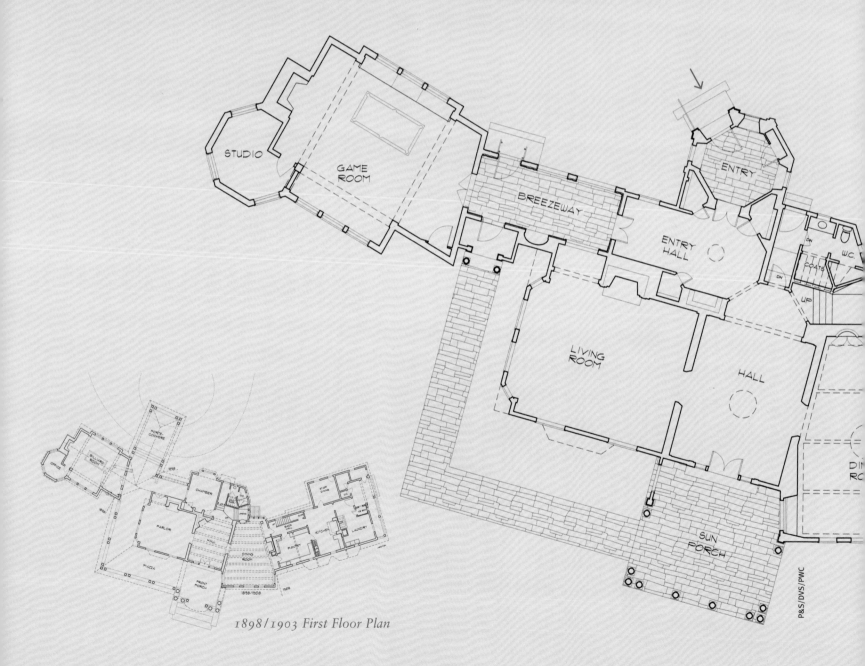

1898/1903 First Floor Plan

It was at this time that the Porte-Cochère was also removed, and the entrance on the north was moved from the breezeway to a new octagonal vestibule. The entry vestibule, Hall, and Living Room all received paneling with classical detailing. These design changes were probably drawn up by J. Lawrence Mauran, a classically oriented architect working in St. Louis, who had a summer house nearby. The tall columns from the front porch were carefully removed and floated across the lake to a site that featured an outdoor amphitheater for summer dance and theater extravaganzas.

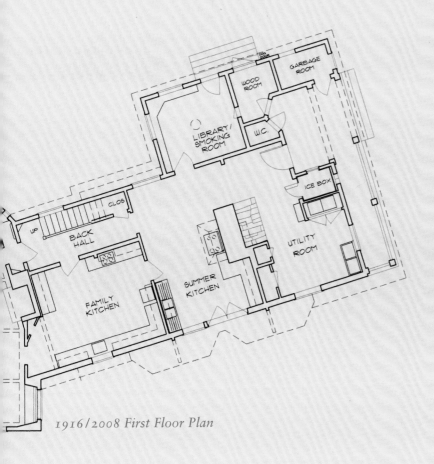

1916/2008 First Floor Plan

Stonlea's original columns served as a fitting backdrop for the many dance and theater productions at an amphitheater across the lake. They still stand today in their weathered elegance.

Another major alteration was the removal of the broad roofs, floors, knee walls, and short columns of the summer porches. The Living Room became significantly brighter, but visually the west side of the main façade lost its broad base. The living patterns of the old house were radically altered with the loss of about 1,500 square feet of outdoor living space. The living room/master bedroom block, with its large bay window and dramatic roofline, was strong enough to hold the composition together. The front porch, that had been elevated was lowered to the ground and paved with flagstones to become the Sun Porch.

Stonlea, 1891

DPL: HDA

Stonlea, 2008

MacM

Stonlea, 2011

1916/2008 Kitchen Wing Plan

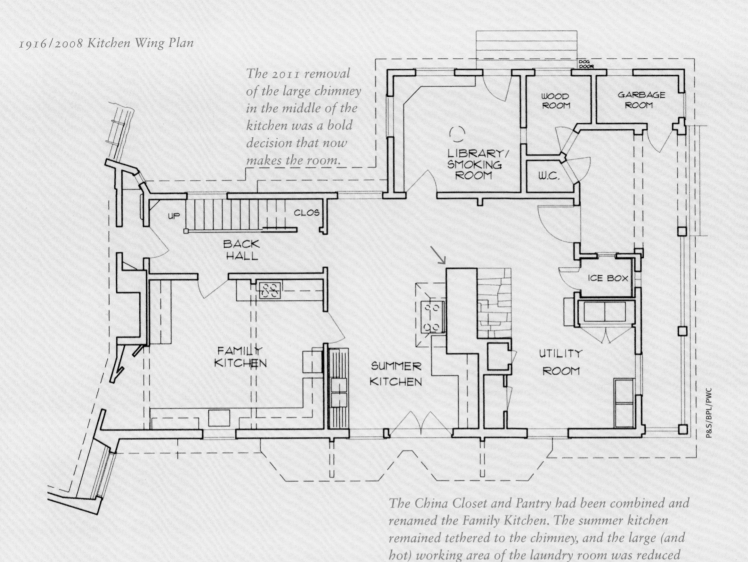

The 2011 removal of the large chimney in the middle of the kitchen was a bold decision that now makes the room.

WOOD ROOM

GARBAGE ROOM

LIBRARY/ SMOKING ROOM

W.C.

UP

CLOS

BACK HALL

ICE BOX

FAMILY KITCHEN

SUMMER KITCHEN

UTILITY ROOM

DOG DOOR

P&S/BPL/PWC

The China Closet and Pantry had been combined and renamed the Family Kitchen. The summer kitchen remained tethered to the chimney, and the large (and hot) working area of the laundry room was reduced by the forces of progress to a closet for the washer and dryer, and some vestigial tubs.

East wing with two chimneys, 2008

East wing with kitchen chimney removed, 2011

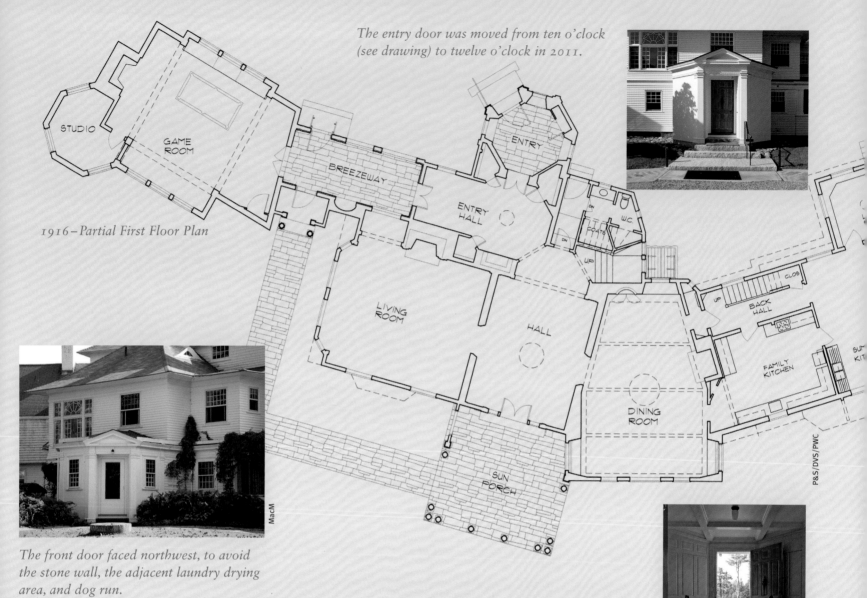

The entry door was moved from ten o'clock (see drawing) to twelve o'clock in 2011.

1916–Partial First Floor Plan

The front door faced northwest, to avoid the stone wall, the adjacent laundry drying area, and dog run.

Octagonal entry vestibule, 2011

The original entry point to the house was at the front porch, through the Hall. The entry moved west when the Porte-Cochère and breezeway were built. In 1916 an octagonal vestibule was built in front of the first office, and a partial octagon in the new Entry Hall was shaped by paneling. The result was new closet space, as well as an ordered entrance progression.

The entry door to the octagon was oriented northwest, due to the close proximity of the back-of-the-house grounds behind the stone wall. When the wall was removed in 2011, the door migrated around to the north, perfecting Mauran's symmetrical plan.

The original fireplaces in the Hall and the office were removed, and the addition of paneling gave the house a more formal look. The angled portion of the Billiard Room makes more sense when you consider that it was fitted in next to the summer porches, now gone.

The small photo above, from 2011, shows the 1916 trim over doorways in the breezeway. It appears over the alcove window, right, suggesting that the alcove was once a doorway.

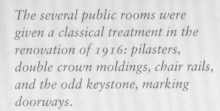

The several public rooms were given a classical treatment in the renovation of 1916: pilasters, double crown moldings, chair rails, and the odd keystone, marking doorways.

The panels in the vestibule form deep-set windows.

The octagonal entrance was modified to place the entrance door in the north facet. The stone wall dividing the old entry motor court from the laundry yard was removed. New low walls define the arrival area and the approach to the new two-car garage.

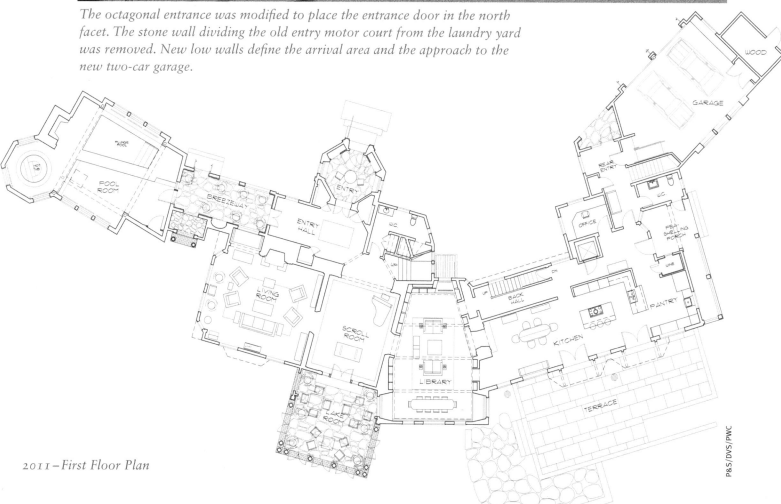

2011–First Floor Plan

the new stonlea
design changes 120 years later

EVERY EFFORT was made to preserve
the existing details, while the energy-saving strategies are
unseen. Life was brought into the house with more
sunlight, open space, striking artwork, livable furniture,
and the artful use of color.

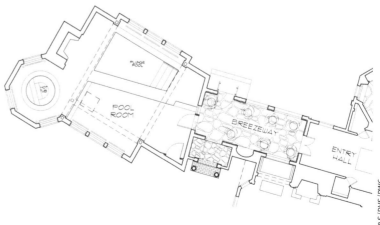

1898–Billiard Room and Office Plan

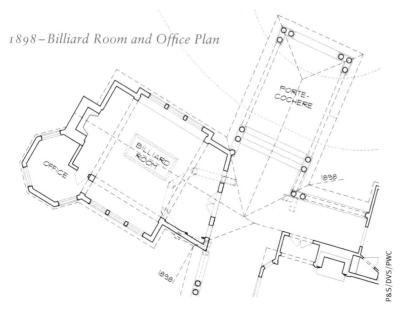

OFFICE

BILLIARD ROOM

PORTE-COCHERE

1898

1898

P&S/DVS/PWC

2011–Pool Room Plan

PLUNGE POOL

HOT TUB

POOL ROOM

BREEZEWAY

ENTRY HALL

P&S/DVS/PWC

The Billiard Room was greatly modified to accommodate a plunge pool, and the Office was opened up for a hot tub. In essence the Pool Room became the Pool Room. The breezeway approach to the pools, that was added when the Billiard Room was built, was enclosed with large panes of glass, to preserve the open look of the original.

The Hall became the Scroll Room, with a collection of Oriental art. The chandelier outlet and rosette were removed, as were the electrical boxes for wall sconces. With the addition of a piano, it continues as a reception area.

The Living Room retains most of the elegant detailed molding and the fireplace mantel from the 1916 renovation.

The Sun Porch was enclosed with mahogany door and window panels, and was renamed the Lake Room. The doors can be hooked open in the summer for an open-air effect, and the space is heated for winter use. The mahogany panels were inserted inside the column system that was built when the house was altered in 1916.

The Dining Room use had changed over time, with the dining table migrating away from the fireplace toward the south windows. Deep, tall bookcases were built into three walls of the room, which became the Library.

The Kitchen area was revised dramatically in the renovation. The chimney separating the laundry area from the kitchen spaces was removed, forming one long space. The Kitchen and Pantry are separated only by cabinetry.

The fireplace in the Library was opened through to the Kitchen. Windows and doors were added that bring in south light and expanded access to the new south terrace.

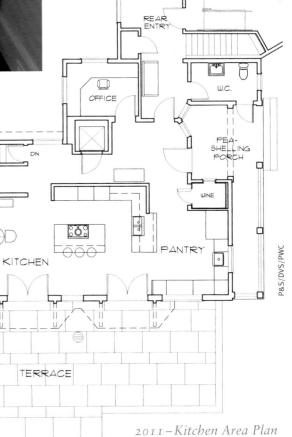

GARAGE

REAR ENTRY

OFFICE

W.C.

PEA-SHELLING PORCH

BACK HALL

UP

DN

WINE

KITCHEN

PANTRY

P&S/DVS/PWC

TERRACE

2011 – Kitchen Area Plan

The second floor was refined to meet the needs of current living, taking down walls and combining small staff bedrooms into spacious guestrooms, a laundry, and bathrooms.

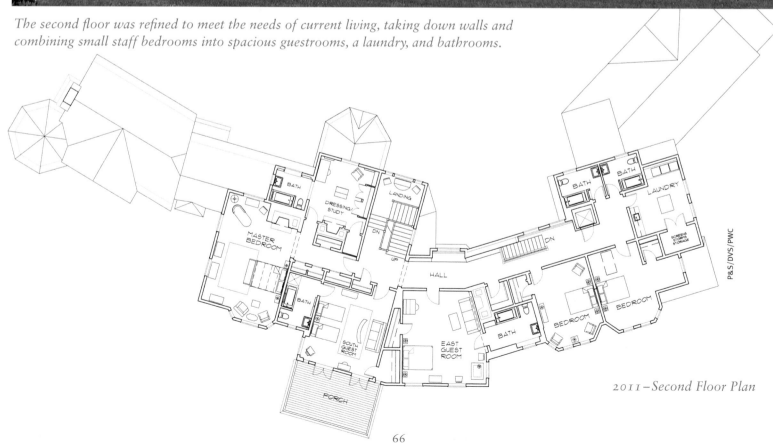

P&S/DVS/PWC

2011–Second Floor Plan

The family bedrooms are a generous nine-feet tall. They are bright, with luxurious bathrooms, closets, and enough room for sofas, chairs, desks, and tables. Each room has a splendid view of the lake and mountain.

The third floor was renovated, and a kitchenette was added. The floor acts as a playroom for great-grandchildren, and as a stand-alone suite.

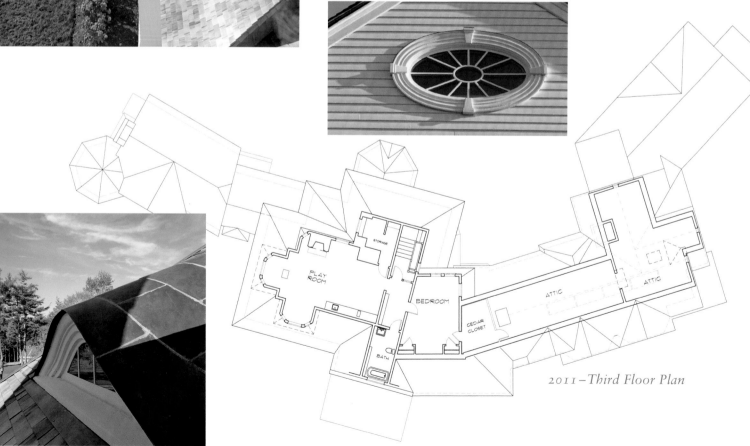

2011 – Third Floor Plan

Third Floor

Playful stencilling highlights the room's role, from the start, as a playroom.

The bathtub behind the oval window has one of the best views in the house.

The area outside of the kitchen, which had been grass, was elevated and paved with large freshwater stones. This terrace, with its easy access back and forth, recognizes that the Kitchen is a center for contemporary life, and is in continuous use.

Exterior

The back of the house was expanded and includes a revised office and a back hall to the driveway and new two-car garage, as well as stairs to a new basement mechanical room. The three bays define the Pea-Shelling Porch, added in 1903. The large arch behind was part of the 1891 design.

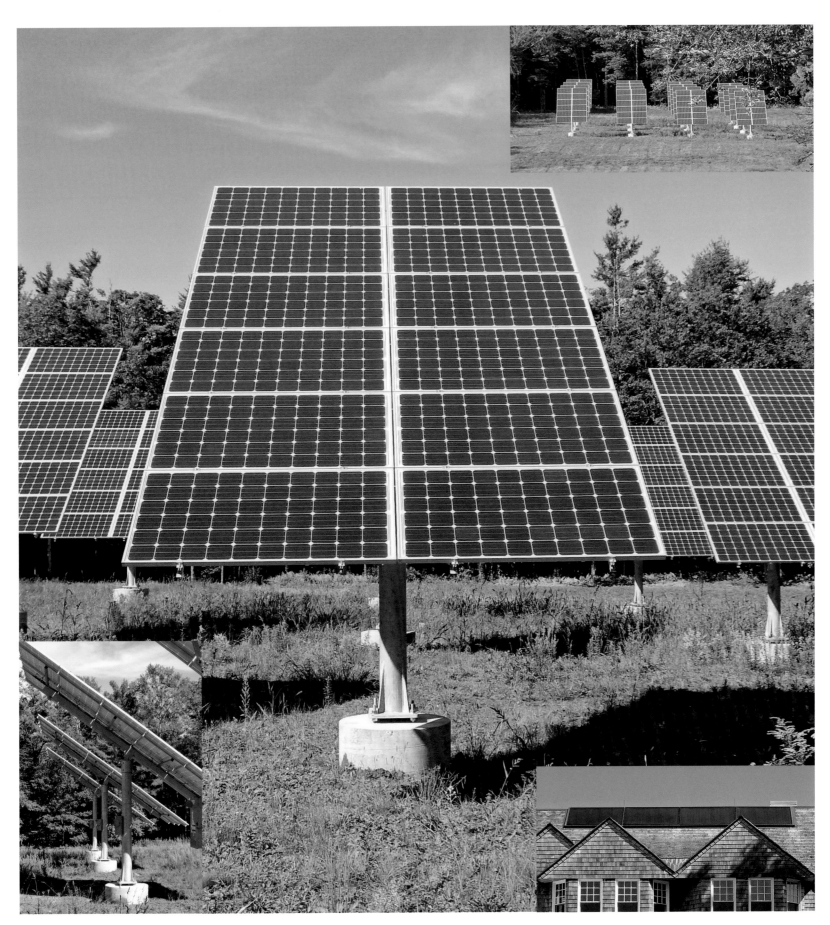

the soul of a house
settled quiet

WHAT GIVES A HOUSE *its "settled quiet?"*

Expanding on the "look and feel" of a house, you might be tempted to use the tricky term the "soul" of the house. Ideally a house has a lived-in quality: It is comfortable; you can navigate easily; it has pleasing proportions; it has varieties of spaces—both sizes and shapes; it has flair: windows of multiple sizes and muntin patterns play with your view. It is what makes you feel at home in your house. It may also be what gives even the visitor a sense of "ownership," making them feel at home there as well.

The term "hearth" comes into play here: The hearth as, literally, fireplace, has long also been the heart of a house. Where does the family gather: in the kitchen, and in front of fireplaces in winter. This was true in colonial times, but with the arrival of the grand house, and the staff to run it, the family was removed from the kitchen. (The builder of Stonlea, it was said, not only never set foot in the kitchen, but wouldn't recognize his cook, walking in town.) The hearth as centerpiece of living in Stonlea was originally in the Hall. The house had an additional seven fireplaces for the family.

Originality plays a part: If the house is a copy of a European model, it may (will) leave the visitor feeling like an art gallery patron—a viewer, and perhaps an admirer, but not a participant. The wingspread theme of Stonlea's layout, highly unusual for its day, gives the house a feeling of connectedness that its more formal compatriots lack. Inside, particularly now with the new opening of the Kitchen wing, you have a sense of what's happening through several rooms. They are not separated by a maze of hallways and walls. The old Dining Room, now Library, has windows that look south to the lake, but also west, into the Lake Room. The cant of the rooms off of each other lends the house an air of informality, as Broadway angles its way through the tight grid of New York City, creating triangular parks, and providing decidedly irregular, and very pleasing, places and views.

". . . [it] has something which he could never get in any new house. It possesses that atmosphere of settled quiet that gathers about old things, while in fact it is hale, hearty and strong."

John M. Carrère

An aerial photograph taken at the conclusion of the renovations, the lake is to the south with Mount Monadnock beyond. The original caretaker's cottage, barn, and stable/garage, are to the left.

SAR

the design process
from the ephemeral to the nuts and bolts

HOW DO YOU BEGIN *to design a large country house, in 1891 or in 2009?*

First of all, what is design? Design is giving shape to something, to a desire. I want to: live in the country in the summer; get out of the sweltering heat of the city; return to my (possibly imagined) agrarian roots; I want to show that I live well, etc.

Many examples of large country houses had been built at various watering holes, notably Newport and Manchester-by-the-Sea, by 1889 when the Catlins visited their St. Louis friends in Dublin.

Seeing an impressive house first-hand is a reliable trigger to wanting one too, and offers an immediate example for inspection. Those who had made the considerable money that would be required to execute such an enterprise, had probably been studying the details of living well, including the trappings, major and minor, for some time.

If you've seen a house that inspires you, from afar, or by visiting it, what do you do next? Talk to the owner, and then find an architect. This involves seeing their work, hearing references, and meeting the firm. These steps were combined in the case of Stonlea: The owner saw the house, bought some land, and hired the same architect, all in August of 1889.

What does the architect want to know from the client, in order to design a custom-made house? These first steps are now known as programming: collecting quantitative information, such as the number of bedrooms; how many children; how do you like to entertain; how many guest rooms? And this being the Gilded Age: What is the makeup of your staff?

An equally important aspect of programming involves teasing out the less measurable but extremely important elements that make up the "look and feel" of the place.

Do you want to express comfort? Does your house blend with the surroundings, or is it made from a more formal palette? Is the family comfortable with "roughing it," in a cottage setting, or does the city follow them into the country?

Until you've talked, at length, with your architect, you may not be aware of some features of a new house that would surprise and please you. Steve Jobs, the founder of Apple Computer, famously said that he didn't design a product according to what people wanted, because, he argued, people don't know what they want. Once you get over the arrogance—implied and expressed—you can see what he was talking about. Until you handled an iPod (assuming you are fond of music) did you know that you wanted one? A good architect can bring fresh insights to the table; suggest alternate ways of solving a design problem; guide you in that unfortunate expression, "thinking outside the box."

Do you want to impress the passerby, and visitors? How formal is the arrangement between family and guests?

An architect once responded to a client's concern over designers' alleged egos (and this from a college professor): "If your architect doesn't have strong opinions, and strong ideas, where are you?" So listen to your new advisors; they will of course bring to bear their own considerable experience of what works, and what has flair. On the other hand, it's a good idea to push back in discussion with your designer: You need to provide guideposts to your ultimate goals, even as they develop. And express your concern over any ideas that don't ring true.

What are some distinctive design features you admire in a house?

There are obviously many precedents to choose from when you consider building a house. What are your contemporaries building? If you are a captain of industry, as the original owner was, you might already be caught up in a serious skirmish for status. A big, second house represents you well in the competitive realm. The large columns in the front of Stonlea were not absolutely necessary, but they did answer to the issue of making an impression.

Monadnock Farms and Stonlea were quite different from each other: one bold and boxy, with simple, strong *fenestration*, and the other more elegant in its classical garb. Given that the same designers worked on both Monadnock Farms and Stonlea, and only a few years apart, you could infer that the personalities of the owners (and their wives) played a part in the design decisions.

Whereas the earlier summer houses in Dublin were shingled and expressed a leafy summer informality, Stonlea was an unusual combination of formality and ease. The original Front Porch is very formal; less of the country than the city. The Piazza, on the other hand, was probably furnished in such a way that adults and children could coexist on rainy days, and where napping was a distinct possibility. The Piazza consisted of two very large roofs, on the south and west sides of the living room, covering an area of about fifteen-hundred square feet. With almost two feet of overhang, all these porches provided cover from the sun (something to be avoided in the nineteenth century), and all but the fiercest wind-driven rain.

Given the enormous columns and proud pediment, badges of classical stature, you might expect the entire house to have a four-square formality. You instead find Stonlea bending with its hilltop contours. From both outside and inside, there is a sense of puzzle parts being assembled, or of a necklace laid down over collarbones: The rooms flow one to the other. The house forms an informal arc, framing an exterior panorama of woodland, fields, lake, and mountainside.

The house also has an interior panorama, of sorts: With the rooms canted obliquely away from each other, you have accidental views into the adjoining rooms. Few other houses of this period have a floor plan that bends off of an orthogonal layout, and provides such a relaxed and charming plan.

The room labeled "Hall" in the 1891 plans conjures up a formal reception area. But the complete label would have been "Living Hall." This room was a popular organizing feature of house plans of the time. It was meant to be a place where the family gathered when the weather precluded being outdoors. Stonlea's Hall originally had a fireplace in one corner, which signaled the room's role as a gathering place. The Living

" . . . now in homes of every size the tendency is to make the hall at once beautiful and useful, the most conspicuous feature in the architectural effect and the most delightful living-room of all; not a living-room like the others [the parlors or drawing rooms], but one with a distinct purpose and therefore a distinct expression of its own. . . . a room which in its uses shall stand midway between the piazzas on the one hand and the drawing-rooms and libraries on the other; perfectly comfortable to live in when the hour means idleness, easy of access from all points outside and in, largely open to breeze and view, yet with a generous hearthstone where we may find a rallying-point in days of cold and rain; in short, a spacious yet cozy and informal lounging-place for times when we cannot lounge on our beloved piazzas."

Mariana Griswold Van Rensselaer

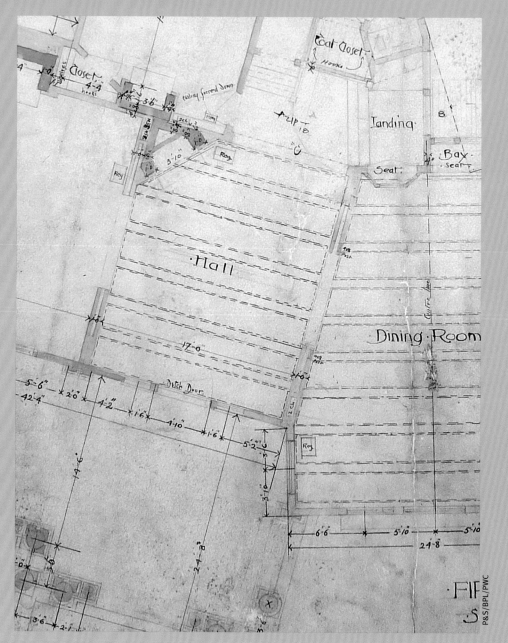

Hall soon gave way to being a ceremonial space, as the "living" competed with traffic flow.

The room labeled "Parlor" sounds like our living room, but was then a more formal space. In a larger house, the parlor was often backed up by a Library, the destination of the men after dinner. Stonlea's Library didn't materialize until seven years later, and then as the Billiard Room.

From the point of view of running a house like this, there were two famous resources to consult: *Mrs. Beeton's Book of Household Management*, (1864), and (take a breath) *The American Woman's Home: Or, Principles Of Domestic Science; Being A Guide To The Formation And Maintenance Of Economical, Healthful, Beautiful, And Christian Homes*, (1869), written by Catharine Beecher and Harriet Beecher Stowe. These two books, one English, and the other American, were immensely influential in their day (Beeton's is continually updated, and is still in print). They answered the need for a map for living a life recently introduced to leisure time, and more disposable income, following the Civil War. While the Catlin family had long ago settled into the requirements and subtleties of running a big house, *The American Woman's Home* was certainly consulted.

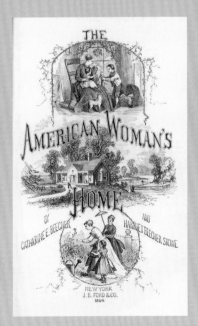

The Misses Beecher

The kitchen at Mark Twain's house. The Misses Beecher, who advised American households, coincidentally lived next door.

Rotten wooden gutters and disconnected downspouts

120-year-old sills

Rotted wood sills and loose stone foundations

repairs

Recording shingles in a "diaper" pattern

5½"

1"

Classical dentil detail meets shingle saw-tooth cladding

Original rosin paper vapor barrier

Loose stone foundation

repairs
courage required

The house had survived for 118 years before the current renovation was undertaken. It is remarkable that it survived intact for so long. The difficulties inherent in maintaining and improving a house, particularly one of this size, include:

MODERNIZING THE BASIC SYSTEMS, OVER TIME

Introduction of electricity and interior plumbing: threading new wiring and plumbing through the house without compromising the interior and exterior design.

New kitchen requirements: wood-burning stoves to electric to propane; icebox to electric refrigerators and freezers; fire-heated water to dish-washers. The running of the kitchen moved out of the hands of a large staff and into the hands of the family.

Laundry requirements: wood-fired water heating to electric or propane-fired or solar-heated hot water; laundry tubs and washboards and wringers to electric washers and dryers. The staff was reduced as these "labor-saving devices" became more prevalent.

Addition of heat: extending the habitable season, or making it a year-round house. The original drawings show a furnace in the "Deep Basement" under the Dining Room, with two "Radiators" (floor grills) in front of fireplaces.

Septic system upgrades from a cesspool to a modern septic tank and leaching field system, as well as drilling a new well.

Deferred Maintenance: correcting long term damage to the fabric of the building. Stonlea was used only as a summer house until sometime in the mid-twentieth century. While this resulted in less wear and tear, it also made fewer demands on the family to provide up-to-date improvements. And it meant that the house was empty and less-closely monitored for nine months of the year: A roof leak could go undetected for enough time that significant damage could result.

AREAS OF REPAIR IN 2009

The *sills*: the course of wood (10" x 10"+ / -) that sits on the foundation and provides the base of the wall structures. Sills are vulnerable to rot when the original foundations are informally laid stone, and surround a *crawlspace* that can trap moisture. Stonlea's sills were severely damaged. Repairs involved propping up portions of the wall and patching in new, treated pieces of wood.

The sheathing and clapboards: Removing the old clapboards and shingles revealed red *rosin paper* that was used as a liner, much as *felts* or housewraps are used today. The siding was removed and disposed of appropriately, since it was painted with lead-based paints. It was all replaced, with clapboards and shingles distributed in their original hierarchy: clapboards on the main house, and shingles, with a base of clapboards, on the east wing.

The copper *flashing* around windows, doors, and roof eaves was replaced.

The roof structure: The board *sheathing* was removed, and the rafters repaired where necessary. New plywood sheathing was installed.

Chimneys were repointed, and caps were repaired. Where allowed by code, chimney-top dampers were installed to prevent warm room air from escaping when the fireplace was not in use. The east chimney was demolished to make room for the more open kitchen and pantry, as well as more open space on the second floor.

Energy-conserving strategies

Thoroughgoing insulation of foundations, walls, and roofs; prevention of air infiltration; introduction of insulating glass in the windows; moisture prevention; window, chimney, and roof flashing improvements.

Rotted sills and stud bases

Open breezeway on north side of house

The clapboards and the underlying sheathing were removed, leaving the studs and interior finishes untouched. The diagonal members provide wind bracing for the house. The deep band of wood above the living room windows was the nailing point for the original Piazza roof that wrapped around from the south to the west.

Chimneys were repointed, and caps were repaired. A chimney-top damper was installed over the one wood-burning fireplace. New Hampshire codes don't allow dampers over gas-fired logs, which account for the rest of the fireplaces.

The sheathing and clapboards were being removed to reveal little or no insulation. Note earlier shingles in a bilious green color.

Roof repair and rebuilding. Note the 1891 dormer, with its old shingles, enclosed by the larger 1903 dormer.

Irregular spacing of studs made it difficult to install substantial amounts of new insulation.

P&S/DVS/PWC

the roof

Architects and builders spend a large portion of their problem-solving skills on fighting off the great enemy of the built environment: *water*.

Sources include water in the ground, rainwater (straight down), wind-driven rain (horizontal), water in the air (humidity, natural and bathroom-shower-made). Life-giving water provides crucial nutrients to us, and our foods, but it also nurtures mold, and the organisms that slowly eat away at wooden roof shingles, rafters, foundations, windows, etc. In a word: rot.

Where to start building a defense against unwanted water? Think of camping overnight: What's the first order of business in setting up a campsite? Putting up a tent: all roof. Roofing of houses has evolved from leaves, to branches, to bark, to hides, to canvas, to boards, to shingles of a variety of materials. Whether made of wood, ceramic, or asphalt, roof shingles have been around for a long time.

An unsung hero of civilization, the wood shingle has operated for centuries on the basis of shedding. The shingles are laid down like an oversized hand of Solitaire, but in reverse. The "hand" is dealt from the bottom up, with the upper shingles (cards) laid over the lower shingles, so a water droplet (or deluge), running downhill, steps down from one to the other, without an opportunity to enter the house. This same principle is at work with a window: The upper sash is mounted outboard of the lower one. The shingles overlap and cover the nails in the lower courses: No nails are exposed to the weather. The Solitaire analogy has one other modification: The horizontal rows of shingles do not line up with the next

Stonlea's new cedar shingle roof and copper valley flashing. The toothed edges are copied from remains of the original roof shingles. They are a decorative flourish, and may speed the draining of the roof, by collecting water droplets to give the flow more gravity.

Copper flashing over door entry

New copper valley flashing, where two roofs converge. Note staggered joints.

Note the "fold" in the roofs.

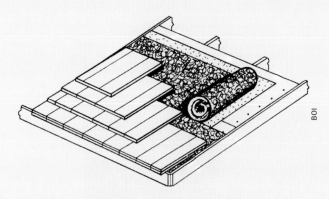
Drawing of Cedar Breather® installation under cedar shingles

Roll ridge vent

row; they have a substantial side lap, so water that could get in is briskly escorted back outside.

With the roof made of more solid sheathing, like planking or plywood, builders began adding a layer of petroleum-saturated paper, known as tar-paper or "felts." Felts allowed for movement between roofing and roof, and provided another defense against water vapor: a *vapor barrier*.

The repairs and improvements to the roof construction at Stonlea included removing the existing layers of roof shingle and substrate (older: wood planking and newer: plywood); repair of the eaves, where water damage is most likely to occur, and rafters; new *tongue-and-groove* plywood sheathing. Next was an application of a bitumen sealer, that offers protection from ice and water (black in the photos). In this case the material was IKO Goldshield®. This layer seals the substrate under a sticky (one side) bitumen layer that will not permit water to enter, and automatically seals around roofing nails. Red cedar shingles were nailed to the sheathing. Under the shingles is a ventilated underlayment, a wiry plastic material, in this case called Cedar Breather® that holds the shingles off the substrate by a quarter of an inch, allowing the shingles to dry out thoroughly.

All the flashing was replaced with copper. The underside of the roof was sprayed with closed-cell foam insulation (see Insulation, page 93).

Detail of Cedar Breather®

A photo of Stonlea from the west that demonstrates the power of the "roofs-cape" in the composition of the house: the dramatic overhanging eaves, the "fold" near the roof edge, the variety of roof pitches. They all give the façade life, even with the summer porches removed.

ROOF DESIGN

Aside from the important task of weatherproofing the house, the roof is a powerful design element. Peabody & Stearns designed many summer houses between 1886 and 1916, and the roofscape was always an important element in their designs. Stonlea has several prominent roof elements: the bold, nearly three-foot overhang, beyond the face of the building; the change in the pitch of the roof within four feet of the edge (it flattens slightly); the complex collision of roofs that cover the major blocks of the building; the use of dormers and eyebrow windows to spell out the hierarchy of the spaces inside, and in some cases to provide headroom. An unusual detail involved using clapboards or shingles to clad the horizontal *soffits* of the large overhangs.

Here the gables are colliding into each other, the top floor's shingles are stepped out from the lower façade. The east end of the house features a dramatic swoop of roof that covers a portion of the Pea-Shelling Porch, possibly the entry point to the porch after the 1903 expansion.

MacM

. . . just back from the dry cleaners.

The first step in repairing the skin of the building was to remove the windows and the old siding and sheathing. The window openings were protected from the weather by the remaining storm windows (soon to be jettisoned), and the walls were protected with plastic sheeting. Prior to insulating, rewiring was also done from the outside.

Foam insulation (green) was sprayed into the wall cavities. This layer varied in coverage due to an unanticipated number of wood studs in the wall. This variation would have led to less insulating value, if not for the rigid insulation, applied next.

MacM

92

insulation

The purpose of insulation is to prevent cold air from migrating, or blowing, into the house in winter, and similarly, hot air and heat from the sun in summer.

The basic element of insulation is dead air: air trapped in the makeup of colonial-era "noggin," later Cabot's eel grass quilts, then mineral wool, glass wool (*batt insulation*), urethane foam (open-cell and closed-cell), etc. The denser the material (and the better attached it is to the wall cavity), the better it acts as insulation.

Stonlea was built with no insulation, as it was intended to be a summer house. Later generations of the family began to use the house in the shoulder seasons—fall and spring—and later still for skiing outings. In cooler weather, the east wing was closed-off, up and down, and heated.

The spacing between Stonlea's studs was irregular: There was more wood per square foot of wall than you would expect in modern construction, which cuts down on the effect of *sprayed-in insulation*. To make up for this, a layer of ¾-inch-thick rigid insulation was applied (blue in the photo on page 94) to the studs. Over that, the new plywood sheathing was applied. This thickening of the walls could have overrun the existing window detail, but the new trim was applied within the limit of the old siding (see Windows, page 99).

The measure of a material's ability to resist heat flow—its "thermal resistance"—is called its *R-value*. A heavily insulated 2" x 6" wall can achieve an R-value of R-19. The combined application of foam and rigid insulation brought the R-value of the wall to R40 from R5; the value of the roof to R40 from R10; the basement and crawlspace to R40 from R0.

Insulation had been blown into some walls, but had limited effect since there were obstacles in the walls that prevented them from being filled completely.

The ceiling plaster in this room was removed after the insulation was sprayed from the outside. Steel was added to make up for an old plumbers-vs-carpenters situation: Some time ago, important roof support framing was cut away to allow for piping to be run. This roof had been held up by what head-shaking structural engineers call "habit."

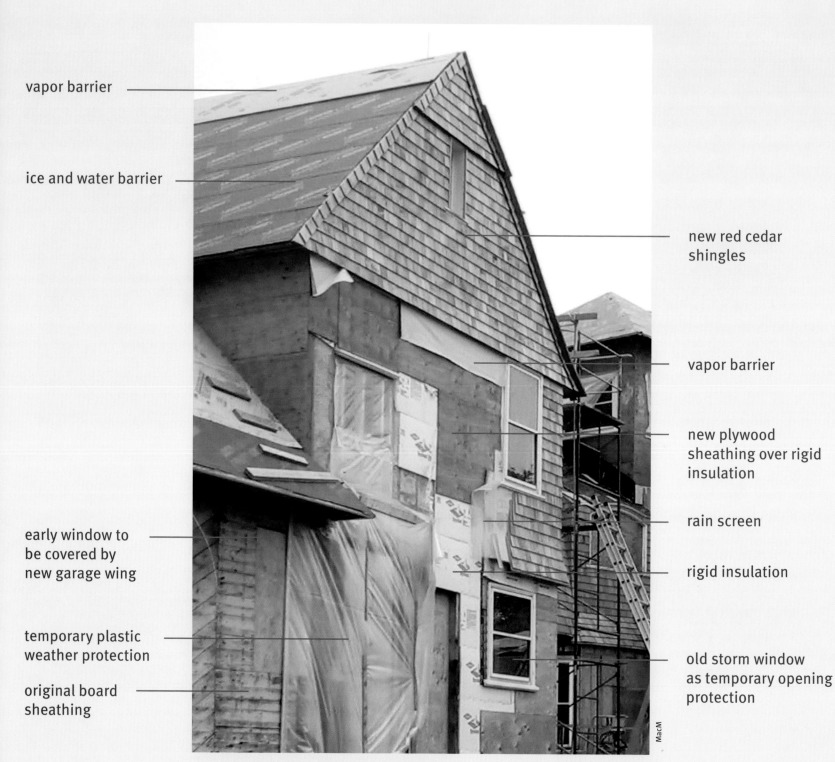

vapor barrier

ice and water barrier

new red cedar
shingles

vapor barrier

new plywood
sheathing over rigid
insulation

rain screen

rigid insulation

early window to
be covered by
new garage wing

temporary plastic
weather protection

old storm window
as temporary opening
protection

original board
sheathing

MacM

This photograph, taken as the new garage was about to
be connected to the old house, conveniently displays
multiple steps in the waterproofing process.

siding

In addition to the roof, the house walls had to be repaired to prevent water from entering: in liquid form, or as vapor.

New waterproofing and insulation were combined to turn Stonlea from a summer house into an year-round house. The old clapboards and sheathing were removed, while the inside walls were not touched. Foam insulation was sprayed into the cavities between the studs, providing a combination of air infiltration barrier, vapor barrier, and insulation. The sprayed-in insulation is a closed-cell insulation called Icynene® (green in the photo on page 93) that adheres to the studs and will not absorb moisture.

Moisture can travel into or out of a house through the walls, carried on air currents or pushed by uneven pressure on one side or the other. Moist air migrates out of the house through the plaster wall finish and into the wall cavity on its way out of the building. If the wall cavity is cold, the moisture will condense, on the insulation or on the outside wall, and the accumulated moisture can cause mold to form and damage the finishes on both sides of the wall.

Combined moisture and vapor barriers, such as the sprayed-in insulation, housewrap, and rain screen (not to mention the shingles), prevent moisture from migrating through the wall.

Signs of wear on the exterior wall of Stonlea, 2009. Water vapor was migrating out from the inside, pushing off the paint, and allowing surface water to penetrate. The lower roof at the far right was painted to look like siding, a classic gambrel roof misunderstanding: If it's vertical, it's a wall; if it's sloping, it's a roof, and should be sided accordingly, as it was in the renovation. Note the flair in the wall at the head of the windows on the first floor.

Carpenters' notes, towards the reconstruction of the original siding patterns

The old siding is being dismantled; the white clapboard was farthest outboard, then the red rosin paper, acting as a vapor barrier, then wood board sheathing against the wall studs. The triangular piece of wood forms the flair at the division between first and second floors.

Home Slicker® as applied under wall shingles or clapboards

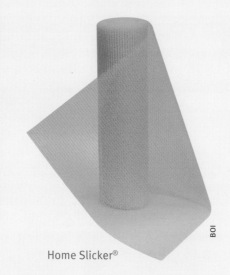

Home Slicker®

A blower door set-up in the hall

The rain screen is a product called Home Slicker® (yellow in the photos), a membrane with small fibrous corrugations molded into it to guide away moisture that might soak through the clapboards or shingles.

AIR INFILTRATION

Older houses leak air: The joints between assemblies like the windows, the walls and roof eaves, or the foundation and the first floor, fit loosely. Wind can blow right through a house, more or less, depending on what steps have been taken to seal it.

To measure the extent of cold air infiltration in winter, or warm air infiltration in summer, tests are now available using a *blower door*. The windows and exterior doors are closed, and the interior doors are opened. The blower door is fitted into the front door opening. The fan (the bottom circle) runs for a period of time, and sensors record the effort required to power the fan: If the house is tight, the fan works harder; if the house is loose, the fan has an easier time pulling in outside air through the chinks in the house's armor.

The air infiltration before the renovation was measured at 12.50 *ACH*50. After the renovation it was measured at 5 ACH50. This reduction in permeability was accomplished by adding tight and efficient insulation between the studs and roof rafters; adding more rigid insulation to the studs; taping over all joints in the window assemblies; refitting the windows with insulating glass with a tighter fit than the original individual glazing; spraying the top of the foundations with thick insulation; and adding a moisture barrier to the roof sheathing to block air as well as water.

08/02/2010 15:12

MacM

The house has received its sprayed and rigid insulation. You can see the difference between modern plywood sheathing, right, and old board sheathing on the left. The plywood adds rigidity to the house that board sheathing cannot replicate.

The Palladian window over the original entrance

The Palladian window on the Peabody & Stearns drawings. The dashed red lines show the layout of the stairs behind. The drawings are a combination of working drawings (blueprints) and presentation drawings. The colorist was highly skilled.

48x27

The Master Bedroom bay window. This drawing shows the distinctive muntin pattern used in the original larger windows.

A photograph of the Master Bedroom window in 1893

windows

The original windows at Stonlea were good examples of how the Colonial Revival style brought variety and interest to the façade of a house.

The windows were an elaborate collection of shapes. They are called out, in this case as 11/1 (said "eleven over one"). In 1916 they were replaced with a simpler, and duller, 18/3. There is a large surviving Palladian window arrangement at the main stairwell, on the north side, a nicely proportioned oval window in the main gable, and several eyebrow windows that add some dash on the third floor.

The original owner on the Front Porch. The arched window muntins were a feature of all of the original large window sashes.

The basic window muntin layout was distinctive, as you can see in the photo of the original owner, sitting on the Front Porch. The shutters were operable, and were closed in the winter to protect the windows.

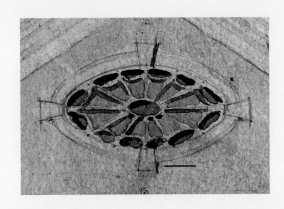

Of all the aspects of the fabric of a building, the windows are most vulnerable to wear and tear, since they are opened and closed often, and present a fragile defense against water: the glazing putty (or wood stops) that holds the panes in place. The putty degrades in the sun over time, and crumbles, letting in water that rots the muntins and sash. In the 1916 renovation, the 1891 window sashes were replaced. The original muntin patterns were replaced with a more regular 18/3 pattern, with no curved elements. When the house began to see winter use, storm windows were mounted on the house, and by then, the shutters had been removed.

Stonlea from the south, shortly after completion. Note the arched window patterns in the larger windows, the oval window in the main gable, and the shutters.

DPL: HDA

1891 windows

2011 windows—the summer porches are gone.

A new 18/3 window
in the Kitchen

In both the 1891 windows and the 1916 windows, each small opening in the sash held one pane of glass, or *light*. This arrangement is termed *"true divided lights."* A single pane of glass has very little insulating value. It doesn't keep out the cold very well, and an old frame allows cold air leaks.

The extra thickness of the 1891 sashes was replicated in the 1916 renovation to allow the new sash to work in the original frames. This allowed for a major improvement to the efficiency of the sashes in the 2011 renovation, by allowing for the insertion of thicker insulating glass in the existing sash.

In the 1970s, when energy saving became an important component of new construction and renovation, it became standard practice to make windows with *double-glazed* (originally called "Thermopane") units. Two pieces of glass are separated by a stop around the perimeter, and the three components are sealed together. The void between the panes is either a vacuum or filled with an inert gas, to prevent condensation.

Replacing multiple small panes in a sash with insulating glass, while giving the windows an authentic look, would be very expensive, and the thicker panes would require thicker muntins, spoiling the *profile* of the window.

A typical upper sash at Stonlea, which had 11, then 18 panes, now has one double-glazed unit of glass. The insulating glass has matching muntins on the inside and outside to give the look of the traditional window while making the assembly less expensive to fabricate. Use of insulating glass in this way is called *"simulated divided lights."*

New window with elaborate detail extrapolated from the original house

In the case of Stonlea, the multiple panes were removed. Inside the dividing portion of the sash, the muntins were ground off, leaving only the exterior "checkerboard" pattern. The perimeter seat for the glass was routed out to accommodate the new, thicker glass. The insulating glass was seated over the existing muntins, while new matching muntins were attached to the other side of the glass. The new pane is ⅝-inch thick, vs. the ³⁄₁₆-inch original.

Double-glazing improves the insulating value by a factor of ten. The improvement of double- over single-glazing is typically increased by taking several further steps: the use of *Low-E glass*; the reseating of the sash with interlocking metal weatherstripping called "jamb liners"; the replacement of *counterweights* with coiled spring balances; and by filling the obsolete weight pockets with insulation. The entire assembly was taped to prevent air infiltration.

Storm panels or storm windows, were made to fit on the inside of each window frame, making the window "triple-glazed" and raising the insulating value further. They are mounted inside for ease of changing, and to avoid losing the outside view of the muntins to reflections. In summer the storm panels are replaced with insect screens. Several closets were designated to house the off-season units.

A refurbished window, from the inside: You see the window trim; the window jamb, with screws to allow for sash removal; new sash tape, replacing the heavy counterweights; the sash, with a shadow indicating the two panes of the insulating glass. The sawtooth pattern is cut out of the last course of shingles over the window opening.

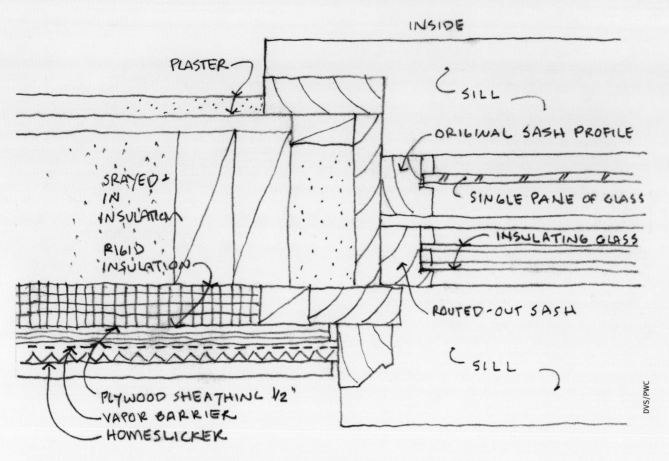

A view of the window construction, cut horizontally (looking down). In the picture both original and improved sashes are shown. The original, above, shows the single pane of glass in the thicker-than-normal sash. The reconditioned sash, below, shows the new double-glazing. Note the different-sized cutouts in the two sashes.

View of the inside of a window after the renovation. Note the storm panel, held in place with metal pins in the jamb. The same pins hold the screens in the summer. The grill in the window sill covers heating radiators.

A sample window, cut through the lower sash. The track to the left is for the upper sash.

. . . cut through the jamb.

. . . cut through the sill.

Wood Windows

brick mold (general shape and dimension)

casing

jamb

blind stop (dimension)

stop

parting bead

sash top rail (height and putty bevel)

muntin (shape, width, and depth of exterior)

meeting rail (height)

putty bevel (depth: dimension from the sash face to the glass surface)

sash bottom rail (height)

sill (height and slope)

sash

lug

(distance from wall face to window)

NPS

Another view of the improved window sash, shown on a full-size mock-up of the window construction. The two panes of glass that make up the double-glazing are visible as black lines, along with the gray sealant. The sash has been routed-out to make room for the glazing and the wooden stop.

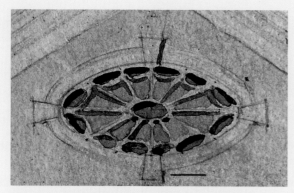

Enlargement from the original Peabody & Stearns drawings. On the drawing, the oval is the size of a nickel.

The Palladian window on the façade of Stonlea in 2009, that replaced the original oval window when the gable was pushed back.

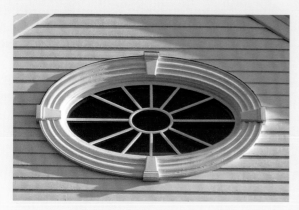

The new oval window

In 1891, even small windows received a flourish.

A detail view of the front porch. Note the stone steps. The door-way to the Hall was a four-foot-wide Dutch door. The side lights visible at the right side of door are wildly decorative. These were replaced with French doors when the Piazza was removed in 1916.

The site plan showing the existing house in white, the garage addition in gray. The centers of the geothermal wells are indicated by the circles, and the PV panels are shown in blue. The circles indicate the area necessary for each well to recover heat from the earth without interfering with the next well.

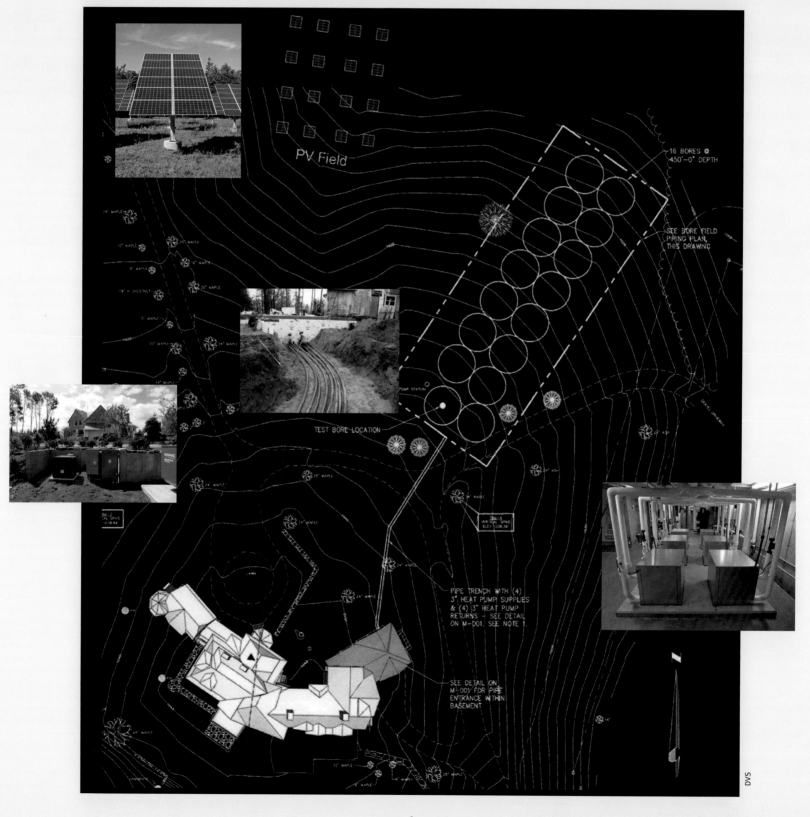

the mechanical systems

towards net zero

The decision was made to make Stonlea a net-zero house—a house that provides for its own electrical energy needs, trading electricity supply and demand with the local power company (the *grid*) to achieve, at the end of a calendar year, zero demand on the grid.

This result is a combined effort of on-site power generation (using *photovoltaic* or "PV" cells) and power conservation (heavy-duty insulation, double-glazed windows, air-infiltration defense), along with geothermal heat pumps, to draw heat from the earth, and a solar-assisted hot water supply.

THE ELECTRICAL SYSTEM

Basic to Stonlea's net-zero design is the *photovoltaic array* in a field behind the house that is designed to produce electricity for 100 percent of the needs of the house. Usually PV design accounts for 17 percent of the design load, or demand, of the house, so increasing the capacity to 100 percent was a bold decision.

The electrical demand was calculated, assessing the predicted loads:

1. The square footage of the house requiring heat; factoring in the new insulation, windows, and roofs.

2. The heat pump operating loads: The work of pumping the refrigerant into and out of the sixteen 450-foot-deep wells.

3. The standby hot water heating, including storage tanks.

4. The pumps supplying hot water to the radiant heat in the floors, and to the wall radiators.

5. The lighting.

6. The laundry and kitchen loads.

7. The plunge pool and hot tub water pumps, the booster heaters, and the mechanical room dehumidifier.

Close up of solar panels in field

A single PV cell

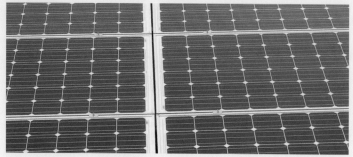
A PV module: a collection of PV cells.

The predicted electrical demand was determined to be 48,000 watts, or 48 kilowatts, or 48kW. To supply that much power, there are sixteen panels in the field north of the house. Each panel is made up of twelve PV modules, each of which are capable of generating .25kW of electricity. The stands supporting the panels are fixed, and the panels are positioned to face the ideal direction, at the ideal angle, to catch the most sunlight for Stonlea's latitude. The angle is manually adjusted for summer and winter.

The PV array is not always able to produce the required power (due to cloudy days, nightfall), in which case a transfer switch automatically brings power in from the local utility grid. Conversely, when the array is turning out more power than can be used by the house, the excess is transferred back to the grid. The result of this trading ideally nets out at no annual cost to the owner.

A PV panel: a linked collection of PV modules.

A PV or solar cell works in three steps:
1. Photons in sunlight hit the solar cell and are absorbed by semiconducting materials, such as silicon. 2. Electrons (negatively charged) are knocked loose from their atoms, causing an electric potential difference. Current starts flowing through the material to cancel the potential and this electricity is captured. Due to the special composition of solar cells, the electrons are only allowed to move in a single direction. 3. An array of solar cells converts solar energy into a usable amount of direct current (DC) electricity. [adapted from Wikipedia]

The small solar farm (a PV array) at Stonlea consists of sixteen fixed solar panels.

Inverters in the basement that collect the DC power from the photovoltaic panels, and convert it to AC power for the house.

inspiration

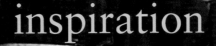

Polly imagined that the PV panels could be arranged to look like armored Samurai warriors in orderly array, reflecting the sun as they prepare to do battle with the dreaded Grid.

Polly's great-granddaughter reviewing her troops, in 2012.

THE HEATING SYSTEM

The house is heated by hot water from six *ground-source heat pumps* that runs through the house in two distribution systems: wall-hung radiators and radiant-floor tubing.

There are sixteen heat pump wells to the north of the house (see site drawing on page 106). Each well was drilled down to 450 feet. A fluid, called a refrigerant, is pumped through two-inch-diameter piping down to the bottom of the wells, and back up, picking up heat from the earth as it travels. On the site, testing revealed that the ground temperature at that depth was 50°F.

On a 0° day in the winter air, the fluid is pumped into the wells where it is warmed to 50° and returned to the new basement where it runs through one of six heat pumps. If the house is to be heated to 70° while the outside temperature is 0°, the heating effort is given assistance by the heat pump, less transfer loss.

The six ground-source heat pumps in one of the new basements.

In the case of Stonlea, the pumps form an "asymmetrical system," since they are not providing air conditioning. They are borrowing heat from the earth all winter, but not returning it through the reverse air conditioning process in the summer, so the earth needs time to recover its base temperature. To assist in this, the wells were drilled on twenty-five-foot centers, instead of twenty-foot centers.

What does the heat pump itself do to "create" heat? The household refrigerator is a good model for comparison: It moves heat out of the food storage compartment to the coils on the back, or top of the unit, where it is disbursed into the room.

The refrigerator (and the heat pump) contains the following components:

1. **Compressor**: increases the pressure of the refrigerant vapor (red), pushing it through the system (up the back of the refrigerator), and increasing the vapor's temperature above that of the surrounding kitchen. The heat is thrown off the metal coils, into the air.

2. **Condenser**, or coils, are usually behind, or on top of the refrigerator, where the refrigerant vapor condenses to a liquid.

3. **Expansion valve**: causes a sudden drop in refrigerant pressure, causing it to boil, contradictorily causing a temperature drop. This valve is like the can of compressed air: when the valve releases the pressure of the (red) refrigerant, its temperature drops (blue).

4. **Evaporator**: coils inside the refrigerator, that draw the latent heat of the box via refrigerant vaporization (blue to red).

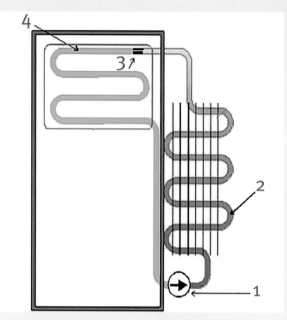

A cross section of a refrigerator. Reverse the process: red inside, blue outside, to heat the house.

The key to understanding this process is to know that when vapor is condensed, it heats up; and when pressure on it is released, it cools. If you've filled balloons for a party with an air compressor, you've probably burned yourself on the compressor: It gets *hot*. When you use a spray can of compressed air, to clean computer keyboards or camera lenses, you'll notice that the can becomes cool: The released pressure causes the propellant in the can, that is pushing out the air, paint, etc., to boil, counterintuitively, drawing in heat from the contents and the can.

The heat pump assembly at Stonlea operates like a refrigerator, but in reverse. The heat produced by the basement compressors is run through the house, and is given off by the fins and coils in the radiators. The cooler liquid is returned to the pumps and run back into the ground, to pick up the temperature-raising assistance of the earth (50° at 450 feet below grade). The approximately 50° liquid is then run through the compressors again, where the temperature is raised to approximately 110°, for its run back through the house.

Heat Distribution – Wall Radiators

Radiators are the descendants of the large, heavy, often clanking, cast-iron beasts familiar to everyone born before 1970. Some of these old units heated the east portions of the house that the previous owners kept open in winter. They were made up of hollow sections that were bolted together in numbers specified according to how much heat was required: more sections, more heat. The sections were shaped like elongated donuts. They were sometimes decorated in the casting process, to reduce the effect of a technical invasion into the room. They were heavy, so they retained heat and contributed it to the room long after the furnace cycled off.

The nostalgic, to some, "clank" of an old radiator, was usually made by units that transmitted steam: As steam cools and condenses it forms water that can temporarily block the passage of steam, until enough pressure forms to push the water through . . . with a loud "bang."

Another familiar form of radiator, designed to *remove* heat, is found in the front of water-cooled cars. The engine's heated water runs through a network of tubes and fins, where the wind from the car's motion carries away the heat. In a house, the process is reversed: The tubes and fins shed the heat of the hot water into the room.

In the 1950s a much cheaper form of radiator was developed that consisted of simple copper piping with thin aluminum fins soldered on at frequent, close, intervals. Hot water from the heat pump travels through the pipe, and sheds its heat to the fins, which in turn heat the air surrounding it, and thus to the room. This is called fin-tube radiation providing *convection* heating. The heated air rises, and is replaced by cooler air, drawn into the hot fins. The fins are delicate, and require a cover to protect them, with vent openings top and bottom, to create a current of heat. The box protecting the fins, and helping to create the convection, is typically large and boxy: not an ally to a cleanly designed room.

Cast-iron radiator

Conventional fin-tube radiator. If hidden inside millwork, only the copper piping and aluminum fins are used.

A Runtal radiator at Stonlea, under a window. The fins that transfer heat from the pumped water to the air in the room are hidden behind flat horizontal "tubes" of heavier steel, that themselves contribute heat to the room.

The millwork at the Library window sill houses traditional fin-tube radiation, without the metal cover. On the right, the slot at the base of the cabinet seen beyond, allows cooler air at the floor to be drawn into the wooden cabinet to be heated. The heated air travels up and out of the slots in the window sill.

A more modern and much sleeker version of fin-tube radiator was developed by a Swiss company called Runtal Co., who patented their panel radiator in the 1950s. They gained wider reception in the U.S. as they began to be specified for design-sensitive installations, and as their price began to come down. The typical unit consists of tightly folded, and tougher, vertical metal fins, masked by horizontal flat tubes that also carry hot water.

Various hot water units were used at Stonlea. Standard fin-tube units are hidden in *millwork* under window sills. Many of the Runtal units are mounted on the walls, usually under a window, where most of the cold air is created. They are of a sleek, tidy design and don't call attention to themselves. Another form of Runtal unit is free-standing in bathrooms, where they double as heat sources for the room and as towel warmers. Their fine detailing makes them an addition to the interior design of the bath, rather than a necessary eyesore.

A Runtal room heater and towel warmer at Stonlea

Heat Distribution – Radiant Floors

The radiant floor system consists of loops of plastic or metal tubing under the finish floor. Hot water is run through the tubing, giving off heat through the wood or tile flooring. A wood subfloor is routed to receive the tubing. Return loops and odd-shaped rooms require puzzle-like assembly of the routed wood. Tubing that runs in a concrete-based floor are held in place by ties before the pour.

DOMESTIC HOT WATER

Four large solar panels are mounted on the south-facing roof, and assist in providing domestic hot water (as opposed to hot water for heating the house). In another variation of the radiator, thin tubes of glycol, which won't freeze, are run inside glass-faced panels that absorb the heat from the sun. The liquid runs down to the basement, where its heat is *exchanged* to two large, heavily insulated, hot water storage tanks. These tanks are linked to an equally large and heavily insulated hot water heater, that provides a boost in temperature, as required.

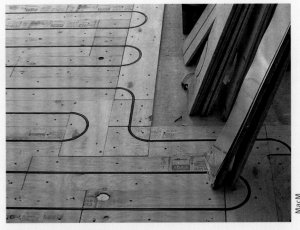

Radiant heat tubing being laid out in wooden subfloor . . .

. . . and in a concrete floor slab pour.

Solar hot water panels on the south roof of the east wing that heat domestic hot water for the entire house.

Solar hot water collector tanks, small pressure tank, and booster tank

LIGHTING

In 1891 the lighting was provided by kerosene lamps. By 1900 electricity had arrived at Stonlea, and sconces and chandeliers were installed that broadcast brighter light from fewer points in the room than we are used to nowadays.

Modern lighting tends to be less aggressive: In this case, recessed downlights and wall washers with three "lamps" (bulbs), call almost no attention to themselves. They are placed in the service of highlighting the features of a room, rather than flooding it with light.

The Hall in 2008 retained much the same appearance it had in the nineteenth century, with a chandelier as the central focus point and additional wall sconces flanking the doors.

Close up of recessed accent light in the library

The same Hall in 2012. Downlights can bathe the room in light, or throw a pinpoint of light in a desired direction.

Landscape lighting in the stone wall

glossary

ACH: Acronym for "Air Changes per Hour." Used to describe the results of a blower door test. 1 ACH means all the air in a house is exchanged once per hour.

ASTRAGAL: A convex molding attached to one or both meeting stiles of a pair of double doors in order to prevent drafts.

BATT INSULATION: A sheet of matted fibers such as cotton, wool, or fiberglass that is used to insulate walls, roofs, and floors.

BELVEDERE: A building, or an architectural feature of a building, designed and situated to look out upon a pleasing scene. From the Italian for "beautiful sight."

BLOWER DOOR TEST: Blower door tests measure how often the total volume of air in the house is replaced with outside air. The results are expressed in "Air Changes per Hour," or "ACH." With a blower door fan running and a house's pressure at negative 50 Pascals (a standard measure), a typical existing home might leak at the rate of 15 Air Changes per Hour, which is written 15 ACH50. Really tight houses can get down to 1 ACH50 or even less.

BREEZEWAY: A covered walkway, alongside a building, or forming a connection between two parts of a building. A breezeway, as its name suggests, allows winds through the space, while protecting the occupants from rain or snow.

BUILDING FABRIC: The surfaces and structure that make up a building: roof rafters, sheathing, waterproofing, shingles, wall studs, insulation, sheathing, clapboarding, floor structure, windows, doors, and so on.

CANTILEVER: A suspended portion of a structure. A diving board is a familiar form of a cantilever.

CHAMBER: The term was used on turn-of-the-century architectural plans to indicate a bedroom, and sometimes to differentiate family bedrooms (usually somewhat grand) from the simpler "bedrooms" of staff.

CLAPBOARD: A kind of wood siding for a house, consisting of long, thin boards that taper from one edge to the other. The boards are attached to the house's sheathing, thin edge up, thick over thin, like long shingles. The word derives from the Dutch word "klappen," "to split."

COLONIAL REVIVAL STYLE: Colonial Revival (also called "Georgian Revival") architecture was an architectural style that sought to revive elements of early American architecture, and that gained popularity in the United States beginning in the late nineteenth century. Features include elaborate front doors, often with decorative crown pediments and overhead fanlights and sidelights; paired and triple window openings; and multi-columned porches.

CONVECTION: The movement of air: Warm air rises, cooler air falls. In the case of a house, refers to the action of air over the warm coils of a heating system.

COTTAGE: Typically used today to describe a small house. In the late nineteenth century, the term also was applied to much larger summer houses.

COUNTERWEIGHT: In older wooden double-hung windows, the heavy object used in a weight-and-pulley balance system to offset the weight of a window sash and allow easy raising and lowering. Counterweights were built into a window jamb assembly, with access doors to allow for repairing the rope or chain used to suspend them. Modern windows use tension systems that don't require elaborate passageways for the weights.

CRAWLSPACE: The space under the first floor of a house, open to the earth or concrete surface below; a space too low for occupation.

DEFERRED MAINTENANCE: The practice, sometimes necessary, of postponing maintenance activities, such as roof repair, furnace cleaning, etc. If left untended, deferred maintenance can eventually result in failures of the systems of a house.

DIAPER PATTERN: A repetitive layout of lapping, lozenge-shaped wood shingles, that form an overall diamond-shape. Often found on Shingle Style houses, as a decorative highlight, an expression of texture.

DORMER: A construction with a gable roof and a window at its outer end that projects from a sloping roof, providing headroom under a pitched roof, or attic. From the French word "dormer," "to sleep."

DOUBLE-GLAZED WINDOW: A window in which two panes of insulating glass are installed in one window sash, separated by an air space or vacuum to reduce the transfer of heat or cold through the unit.

DOUBLE-HUNG WINDOW: A window in which movable upper and lower sashes slide up and down in tracks in the jambs.

DUTCH DOOR: Originally known as a "double-hung door." It consists of two horizontal panels, separately hinged such that the top can be opened separately. Originally designed to keep animals in the stable, and children in the house, while allowing air and light inside. Known as a "stable door" in England.

ELEVATIONS: A drawing that shows the face of the building: the façade. A "North Elevation" refers to an exterior view of the north side of a building.

FEDERAL STYLE: A style of architecture and decoration featuring elements inspired by the classical ages of Greece and Rome. The style became popular in the United States following the American Revolution, between about 1780 and 1830; also called "Late Georgian."

FELTS: An older form of housewrap that provides a layer of moisture protection under the exterior finishes of a house. Also called "tar paper," felts were typically made of heavy-duty paper, saturated with asphalt or tar. They are used between roof sheathing and roof shingles, and can be used in wall assemblies.

FENESTRATION: Pertaining to windows.

FLASHING: Weatherproofing that prevents water from entering a building. Copper, lead-coated copper, and fabric (concealed) are materials used for flashing. Flashing is used at joints, such as roof valleys or the angle between a chimney and a roof, where water can penetrate.

FRENCH DOOR: The term describes a door with glass lights extending its full length. French doors are usually mounted as a pair without a central mullion, or astragal, which allows for free movement of air, light, and people through the doorway. Known as a "patio door" in England.

FRIEZE BOARD: A deep strip of panel on a wall. On an exterior wall, a frieze board is placed above the siding but below the molding at the roof overhang. On an interior wall, it is placed above the picture rail and below the ceiling crown molding. Often decorated with carvings or painted figures.

FURRING: Strips of wood installed behind wall finishes, or under roofing materials, that allow for even support, or for a space behind the construction for ventilation, etc.

GABLE: The triangular part of an exterior wall under the end of a pitched roof, marking the end of that portion of the structure.

GAMBREL ROOF: A symmetrical roof with two pitches to a side: shallow above, steeper below. The design provides additional headroom with a shorter overall height. Sometimes called a "Dutch Colonial" roof.

GILDED AGE: A period of American history from about 1860 to 1900 that witnessed explosive economic growth. The Industrial Age was maturing, and capital accumulated at a great rate. Mark Twain coined the term, referring to the thin veneer of propriety (gold) that covered a multitude of inequities.

GREEN BUILDING: A somewhat overworked phrase that refers to a building constructed with materials and methods that have a low impact on the environment, such as materials that are replaceable, and mechanical and electrical systems designed to conserve energy.

GRID: Refers to the electrical utility distribution system for an area; formerly used to refer to high tension lines, but now used more often to refer to the whole system, as in "selling self-generated power back to the grid."

GROUND-SOURCE HEAT PUMP: Part of a system that uses the earth as a heat source to reduce the cost of heating a building.

GRUBBING: Used to describe the process of clearing plant material, specifically brush, stumps, and roots, from a landscape.

HEAT EXCHANGE: Refers to the transfer of temperature (up or down) between two materials, without the materials touching. A car radiator runs hot water through thin metal fin-tubes so cooler outside air can flow over them and draw off heat.

HOUSEWRAP: A lightweight, synthetic material applied underneath exterior finishes; housewraps prevent rainwater from infiltrating a building from the outside while allowing moisture vapor to escape from the inside.

HVAC: Acronym for "Heating, Ventilating, and Air Conditioning." Pronounced by architects as "H-V-A-C," the term refers to the design and installation of those systems in a building. Pronounced "Aych-Vac" by civilians.

INSULATING GLASS: Glass designed to reduce the transfer of heat or cold. Double-paned (or triple-paned) glazing is separated by a sealed space filled with an inert gas to prevent condensation inside the assembly. Originally called "Thermopane."

JAMB (WINDOW or DOOR): The vertical sides of a door or window assembly.

JAMB LINER: A vinyl or plastic weather strip that fits on the inside of a window jamb to provide a snug fit for a window sash. Jamb liners can house additional hardware such as the springs to keep windows balanced and open.

KILOWATT: A thousand watts of electrical energy; abbreviated kW. Stonlea's capacity is 48kW.

KNOB-AND-TUBE WIRING: Electrical wiring that runs through wall studs via porcelain tubes and is supported inside walls and ceilings by porcelain knobs. Used from about 1880 to 1930, and replaced by more efficient armored flexible cable ("BX" metal-armored cables, and later "Romex" plastic cables.)

LATH: Narrow strips of thin wood mounted closely together on the interior of wall studs and ceiling joists. They are covered with several coats of plaster. The term can also refer to modern replacements, such as expanded metal mesh, and gypsum backing boards.

LEAF (DOOR): Refers to indications for doors in a design document; double doors have an "active leaf," which is used most often, and an "inactive leaf," which usually remains closed. The term can also be used in describing a sliding glass door.

LIGHTS (WINDOWS & DOORS): Refers to the glass or glazing in a door or window frame.

LOW-E GLASS: Low-E, or low-emissivity, glass is treated with an invisible metal or metallic oxide coating, creating a surface that reflects heat while allowing light to pass through. Low-E coatings are proven to reduce energy consumption and increase overall comfort in a building.

MEP: Acronym for "Mechanical, Electrical, and Plumbing." Used in design and construction.

MILLWORK: Construction woodwork, fabricated off-site, and installed with little alteration. May include baseboards, crown moldings, door and window casings, as well as kitchen cabinets, library shelving and storage, etc. Sometimes called "casework."

MULLION (WINDOW): The divider between two complete windows; two casement windows, say, are "mulled" together.

MUNTIN (WINDOW): The divider between adjoining panes of glass within a window sash. Formerly called a "sash bar" or "glazing bar." From the Old French "montant," "monter," "to mount."

NET-ZERO: Refers to buildings that provide for their own electrical energy needs, trading electricity supply and demand with the local power company to achieve, at the end of a calendar year, zero demand on the grid.

PALLADIAN: A reference to designs influenced by the sixteenth-century Venetian architect Andrea Palladio (1508-1580). A Palladian window is typified by a round-topped central window, flanked by side windows.

PANTRY: A storeroom, or space where foodstuffs are stored, on open shelves or in cabinets. In New Hampshire, preferably mouse-proofed.

PARLOR: Nineteenth-century term for a "living room." Usually used for more formal occasions than today.

PEDIMENT: An element in classical architecture consisting of a gable, usually of a triangular shape, typically supported by columns. The triangular area within a pediment is referred to as a "tympanum."

PHOTOVOLTAIC ("PV") ARRAY: A linked collection of photovoltaic panels. Also called a "solar array."

PHOTOVOLTAIC ("PV") CELL: A device that converts sunlight into electrical energy by producing a voltage. Also called a "solar cell."

PHOTOVOLTAIC ("PV") MODULE: A connected assembly of photovoltaic cells. Also called a "solar module."

PHOTOVOLTAIC ("PV") PANEL: A collection of electrically connected photovoltaic modules mounted on a supporting structure such as a stand or a roof. Also called a "solar panel."

PHOTOVOLTAIC ("PV") SYSTEM: A collection of components used together to convert energy from the sun into usable electricity. A basic PV system usually includes a PV panel or an array of PV modules, a power converter (an "inverter"), interconnection wiring, and structural supports for all components.

PIAZZA: A broad, covered porch; the term was popular in nineteenth-century architecture. Highly prized in summer houses, before air conditioning: a place to be outside, in the shade in a breeze, or out of the rain.

PILASTER: A shallow column that is attached to a wall and used for decoration. Pilasters provide visual support, and may conceal structural elements.

PLANS: Architectural drawings that describe the layout of a building, room by room.

PORTE-COCHÈRE: Literally "door-covering." The term refers to a covered carriage entrance at the arrival point of a house: Horse-drawn carriages, and later cars, could draw up under this roof and discharge or take on passengers out of the weather.

PORTICO: A protruding porch, usually a story or more high, supported by columns, that leads to an entrance.

PROFILE: The outline or shape of an object; for example, the profile of a sports car is distinct from that of a pickup truck. The profile of a window sash can refer to whether the muntins are thin or thick.

PROGRAM: A written, and sometimes illustrated, document that spells out what the client wants to accomplish with a project. This is a wish list that can include specific requirements (square footages, so many bedrooms, etc.), and general requirements (the "look" of the building, the atmosphere of the rooms, etc.).

QUEEN ANNE STYLE: A style of architecture and decoration popular in the United States from about 1880 to 1910. Its distinctive features include an asymmetrical façade; dominant front-facing gable; overhanging eaves; round, square, or polygonal tower(s); shaped and Dutch gables; differing wall textures; etc.

R-VALUE: The measurement of a material's thermal resistance or ability to resist heat flow. The higher the R-value, the lower the amount of heat that passes through. Building materials such as insulation and insulating glass are typically rated for their R-value.

RADIANT FLOOR HEATING: A type of heating system in which water or another liquid is heated and pumped from a boiler through tubing laid in a pattern of loops directly under a floor. The warmed floor radiates heat to the people and objects in the room.

ROSIN PAPER: A rosin-treated paper (sometimes called "red rosin paper") formerly used in building construction as an air and moisture barrier. Widely used in built-up roofing systems as a first-layer protective barrier.

SASH (WINDOW): The part of a window that holds the glass panes and can move up and down in the window frame. A "fixed sash" doesn't open.

SECTION / CROSS-SECTION: Refers to drawings that cut through a building: like the view of a doll's house. A "section" of layer cake reveals the cake layers and frosting between. The interior walls, floors, and ceilings are drawn to scale, to judge the size of the project, and to describe interior details, like paneling, cabinets, etc.

SHEATHING: A layer of plywood (modern) or tongue-and-groove boards (obsolete) that enclose the studs making up a wall, or the rafters making up a roof. Sheathing adds rigidity to the wall/roof, and is the surface upon which the finish siding or roofing material is applied.

SHINGLE STYLE: An American style of architecture (named by Yale University architectural historian Vincent Scully) that flourished in the 1880s and 1890s. Simpler in effect than Queen Anne Style, the Shingle Style places more emphasis on volume and less on variety in color and materials. The roof and walls of both the upper and ground floors typically have a uniform covering of shingles.

SILL: The course of wood that sits on a building's foundation and provides the base of the wall structures.

SIMULATED DIVIDED LIGHTS: A modern system of glazing whereby an entire window sash is fitted with a single unit of double-paned, insulating glass. A pattern of multiple muntins is overlaid on both sides to simulate an historic pattern, while reducing the actual number of panes from, say, twelve to one.

SOFFIT: The underside of a projecting part of a building, such as a roof overhang.

SPECIFICATIONS: Written instructions, as opposed to drawings, regarding the materials to be used, and the methods of installation or fabrication to be employed. The drawings may show a window, but the specifications tell the builder what kind of window, what kind of glass, what kind of flashing, etc.

SPRAY-IN INSULATION: Modern insulating method, where a foam is sprayed into joist or stud openings. Provides a thermal barrier, and additionally seal gaps in the construction that can be sources of air leaks.

SUBSTRATE: The layer under a finish material. Roof shingles are nailed to a substrate of plywood sheathing.

SUSTAINABLE: Pertaining to a system that maintains its own viability by using techniques that allow for continual reuse.

TONGUE-AND-GROOVE: Refers to the method of fitting a tongue on one edge of a board into a corresponding groove on the edge of another board. Tongue-and-groove joints allow two flat pieces to be joined firmly together while allowing for small movement. Used with sheathing, flooring, and paneling.

TRUE DIVIDED LIGHTS: A reference to the conventional glazing of window sashes, with a separate, single pane of glass for each sash opening. In a Shingle Style or Colonial Revival house, multiple panes were common. Stonlea has some 11/3 (said "eleven over three") sashes. This means that there are 11 panes of glass in the upper sash, and 3 panes in the lower sash.

VAPOR BARRIER: A layer of material (such as roofing paper or polyethylene film) used to retard or prevent the absorption of moisture into a construction.

VERNACULAR: The design commonly used in a region; i.e., not professional in derivation.

W.C.: "Water Closet" or toilet. The term also designates a toilet room, as opposed to a bath room (bathing room). Originally a nautical term.

WORKING DRAWING: Detailed drawings of a structure, giving precise dimensions and finishes, intended for use by a building contractor. Also know as "contract documents."

PR

bibliography

"A Pioneer in a Great Movement," *The Granite Monthly*, XXXIX, no. 1. Concord, NH: Granite Monthly Company, 1907.

Beeton, Isabella. *Mrs. Beeton's Book of Household Management*. London: S.A. Beeton Publishing, 1861. (Originally titled *The Book of Household Management, comprising information for the Mistress, Housekeeper, Cook, Kitchen-Maid, Butler, Footman, Coachman, Valet, Upper and Under House-Maids, Lady's-Maid, Maid-of-all-Work, Laundry- Maid, Nurse and Nurse-Maid, Monthly Wet and Sick Nurses, etc. etc.—also Sanitary, Medical, & Legal Memoranda: with a History of the Origin, Properties, and Uses of all Things Connected with Home Life and Comfort*.)

Bradbury, Dominic. *New Natural Home: Designs for Sustainable Living*. New York: Thames & Hudson, 2011.

Bryan, John. *Maine Cottages: Fred L. Savage and the Architecture of Mount Desert*. New York: Princeton Architectural Press, 2005.

Bryson, Bill. *At Home: A Short History of Private Life*. New York: Anchor Books, 2011.

Cooke, George Willis. "Old Times and New in Dublin, New Hampshire," *New England Magazine*, August 1899, 745–763.

Denenberg, Thomas Andrew. *Wallace Nutting and the Invention of Old America*. New Haven: Yale University Press, 2003.

Downing, A.J. *The Architecture of Country Houses*. New York: Dover Publications, Inc., 1969.

Downing, Antoinette, and Vincent J. Scully, Jr. *The Architectural Heritage of Newport, Rhode Island, 1640–1915*. New York: Bramhall House, 1967.

Duff, Barbara Ball. "The Dublin Colony." *A Circle of Friends: Art Colonies of Cornish and Dublin*, pp. 9–32. Durham, NH: University of New Hampshire Art Gallery, 1985.

Gill, Brendan and Dudley Witney. *Summer Places*. New York: Methuen, 1978.

Girouard, Mark. *Life in the English Country House: A Social History and Architectural History*. New Haven: Yale University Press, 1978.

Girouard, Mark. *Sweetness and Light: The "Queen Anne" Movement, 1860–1900*. Oxford: Oxford University Press, 1977.

Hale, Jonathan. *The Old Way of Seeing: How Architecture Lost Its Magic (and How to Get It Back)*. Boston: Houghton Mifflin, 1994.

Hawley, Sherwin. "Good Taste in Country Houses," *Country Life in America*, October 1906, 619–620.

Hitchcock, Henry-Russell. *The Architecture of H.H. Richardson and His Times*. Cambridge, MA: The MIT Press, 1966.

Hyman, Tom. *Village on a Hill: A History of Dublin, New Hampshire, 1752–2000*. Portsmouth, NH: Peter E. Randall, 2002.

Ketterer, Stephen J. *Rossiter: Country Houses of Washington, Connecticut*. Washington, CT: Gunn Memorial Library, 2006.

Kidder, Tracy. *House*. New York: Mariner Books, 1999.

Leonard, Levi W. *The History of Dublin, N.H.: Containing the Address by Charles Mason, and the Proceedings at the Centennial Celebration, June 17, 1852, with a Register of Families*. Continued and additional chapters to 1917 by Josiah L Seward. Dublin, NH: The Town Of Dublin, 1920.

Lewis, Arnold. *American Country Houses of the Gilded Age*. New York: Dover Books, 1982.

Mansfield, Howard. *Dwelling in Possibility: Searching for the Soul of Shelter*, Peterborough, NH: Bauhan Publishing, 2013.

McDonough, William and Michael Braungart. *Cradle to Cradle: Remaking the Way We Make Things*. New York: North Point Press, 2002.

Meryman, Richard, Jr. *The Dublin Lake Club: A Centennial History*. Dublin, NH: Dublin Lake Club, 2001.

Moore, Charles, Gerald Allen, and Donlyn Lyndon. *The Place of Houses*. New York: Holt, Rinehart and Winston, 1974.

Morgan, William. *Monadnock Summer: The Architectural Legacy of Dublin, New Hampshire*. Boston: David R. Godine, 2011.

Murphy, Kevin D. *Colonial Revival Maine*. Princeton: Princeton Architectural Press, 2004.

Reed, Roger G. *A Delight to All Who Know It: The Maine Summer Architecture of William R. Emerson*. Augusta, ME: Maine Historic Preservation, 1990.

Robinson, Annie. *Peabody & Stearns: Country Houses and Seaside Cottages*. New York: W.W. Norton & Company, Inc., 2010.

Roth, Leland M. *Shingle Styles: Innovation and Tradition in American Architecture, 1874–1984*. New York: Harry. N. Abrams, Inc., 1999.

Rybczynski, Witold. *Home: A Short History of an Idea*. New York: Viking Press, 1986.

Rybczynski, Witold. *The Most Beautiful House in the World*. New York: Penguin Group, 1989.

Scully, Vincent. *American Architecture and Urbanism*. New York: Praeger, 1969.

Scully, Vincent. *The Earth, The Temple, and The Gods: Greek Sacred Architecture*. New Haven: Yale University Press, 1962.

Scully, Vincent J., Jr. *The Shingle Style and The Stick Style: Architectural Theory and Design from Downing to the Origins of Wright*. New Haven: Yale University Press, 1971.

Scully, Vincent. *The Shingle Style Today: Or The Historian's Revenge*. New York: George Braziller, 1974.

Stern, Robert A.M., ed. *Architecture of the American Summer: The Flowering of the Shingle Style*. Introduction by Vincent Scully. New York: Rizzoli, 1989.

Stern, Robert A. M. *Pride of Place: Building the American Dream*. Boston: Houghton Mifflin, 1988.

Tolles, Bryant F., Jr. *Summer Cottages in the White Mountains: The Architecture of Leisure and Recreation, 1870 to 1930*. Hanover, NH: University Press of New England, 2000.

Van Rensselaer, Mariana Griswold. "American Country Dwellings," *The Century Monthly Magazine*, June 1886, 216.

Van Rensselaer, Mariana Griswold. *Art Out-of-Doors: Hints on Good Taste in Gardening*. New York: Charles Scribner's Sons, 1893.

Van Rensselaer, Mariana Griswold. *Henry Hobson Richardson and His Works*. New York: Dover Publications, Inc., 1969.

Wilson, Richard Guy. *The Colonial Revival House*. New York: Harry N. Abrams, 2004.

Withey, Henry F., and Elsie Rathburn Withey. *Biographical Dictionary of American Architects: Deceased*, pp. 462, 568. Los Angeles: New Age Publishing Co., 1956.

Zaitzevsky, Cynthia, and Myron Miller. *The Architecture of William Ralph Emerson, 1833–1917*. Cambridge, MA: Harvard University Press/Fogg Art Museum, 1969.

Polly would like to introduce the cohort behind this project and book:

Hugh Hardy is a Princeton-trained architect, practicing in New York. He is a Modernist, but he also admires well-crafted architecture of any period. *It was a great experience to work with Hugh on the Glimmerglass Opera House. He brought order to our house in Corning, New York, helping us to move from the simpler house of a young family, to the more sophisticated arrangements of the mature family.*

Daniel Scully is a Yale-trained architect with long experience in New Hampshire. He is equally adept at daring new architecture, sympathetic additions, and renovations. *Dan and his colleague, Katie Cassidy Sutherland, were the cutting edge of the immensely complicated task of pulling a project of this scale together.*

I have always admired Peter and Vicky's individual talents; their "eye," that they so uniquely combine for a project like this. I've loved the ease with which they work together to tell a story verbally and visually. It's been my joy to be included in this collaboration.

Peter Clement is a University of Pennsylvania-trained, practicing architect, who studied with Louis I. Kahn. His interest in the architecture of American houses was piqued by Dan Scully's father, Vincent, at Yale. He applied his knowledge as an English major and architect to the task of recording this project.

Victoria Chave Clement received a Bachelor's degree in art history from the University of Denver, and a Master's degree in graphic design from the Rhode Island School of Design. She has owned and run her own graphic design business since 1986. She has taught part-time at RISD, and in addition to her graphic design career, Vicky is a Kripalu-trained, certified, and licensed Prana Yoga teacher.

And we would like to introduce Polly:

Polly Guth has many facets. New Hampshire-born, she returned home by settling at Stonlea. Polly has long been passionate about issues of sustainability and conservation, as well as many other worthy causes, including enviromental responsibility, social enterprise, reproductive health, media reform, and economic security and justice for women. She is dedicated to establishing lead grants to start worthy programs on the road to self-sufficiency.

Hello

project team

Aerial Photography
Intrepid Aerial Photography
95 Brewery Lane, Suite 22
Portsmouth, NH 03801
603.235.4978

Analyst and Envelope Specialist
S.E.E.D.S.
Sustainable Energy Education &
Demonstration Services
48 Bullard Road
Jaffrey, NH 03452
603.532.8979

Architects
H3 Hardy Collaboration Architecture LLC
902 Broadway
New York, NY 10010
212.677.6030

Scully/Architects
17 Elm Street
Keene, NH 03431
603.357.4544

Construction Manager
MacMillin Company, Inc.
17 Elm Street
Keene, NH 03431
603.352.3076

Electrical and Security
Amer Electric
82 Pearl Street, PO Box 1090
Keene, NH 03431
603.357.8553

Electrical Engineer
Downing Engineering
PO Box 276
Harrisville, NH 03450
603.827.3672

Excavation
Oakridge Excavation. Inc.
32 Interral Way
Dublin, NH 03444
603.563.8295

Interval Construction
PO Box 1106
Dublin, NH 03444
603.563.8660

Garage Doors
Overhead Door of Concord
38 Locke Road #1
Concord, NH 03301
603.224.2280

Geothermal, Plumbing, and Heating
Wilder Plumbing & Heating, Inc.
425 Jaffrey Road #B
Peterborough, NH 03458
603.924.2299

Geothermal Wells
Cushing & Sons Water Well Drilling
Route 12 North
Keene, NH 03431
603.352.8866

History
The Dublin Historical Society
PO Box 415
Dublin, NH 03444
603.563.8545

Dublin Public Library
Main Street, PO Box 442
Dublin, NH 03444

Historical Society of Cheshire County
PO Box 803, 246 Main Street
Keene, NH 03431
603.352.1895

Boston Public Library, Fine Arts
Department, Peabody & Stearns
Collection of Architectural Drawings
(1870–1917)
Third Floor, McKim Building
700 Boylston Street
Boston, MA 02116
617.859.2225

Kitchen Cabinets
Windmill Hill Cabinets
Windmill Hill Road
Dublin, NH 03444
603.563.8503

Kitchen Counters
Creations in Stone
147 South Winchester Street
West Swanzey, NH 03446
603.357.2260

Keene Monument Company
555 Main Street
Keene, NH 03743
603.352.7221

Landscape Architect
Jane MacLeish Landscapes
3743 Upton Street, NW
Washington, DC 20016
202.966.8279

Mechanical Engineer
Kohler & Lewis
27 Mechanic Street
Keene, NH 03431
603.352.4841

Metal Doors and Hardware
Lang Door & Hardware, Inc.
2 Brookside West
Hooksett, NH 03106
603.627.2706

Millwork and Doors
Cox Woodworking, Inc.
703 Route 63
Westmoreland, NH 03467
603.399.7704

Painting and Papering
S & S Painting, Inc.
625 New Hampshire 10
Swanzey, NH 03446
603.358.5594

Stebbins Spectacular Painting
313 Main Street
Marlborough, NH 03455
603.352.1960

Photovoltaic Contractor
Froling LLC
19 Grove Street, PO Box 178
Peterborough, NH 03458
603.924.1001

Pools
Quality Design Nor'easter Swimming
Pools, Inc.
106 Perimeter Road
Nashua, NH 03063
603.880.4888

Patenaude Pool Plasterers, Inc.
PO Box 30
37 Meadow View Lane
Hartland, VT 05048
802.436.2733

Radiant Floors/Solar Domestic Hot Water
Viega Proradiant System
59E Daniel Webster Highway
Merrimack, NH 03054
603.882.7171

Site Engineer
Clough Harbour and Associates (CHA)
11 King Court
Keene, NH 03431
603.357.2445

Stone Walls and Plantings
Simpson Landscape
Monument Road
Dublin, NH 03444
603.563.8229

Stone Foundations and Chimneys
Legrand Masonry
68 Lumber Street
Athol, MA 01331
978.249.7184

Structural Engineer
T.R. Fellows Engineering
PO Box 428
Walpole, NH 03784
802.318.7854

Survey and Septic
SVE Associates
47 Marlboro Street
Keene, NH 03431
603.355.1532

Window Restoration
Window Master
Dublin Sash Systems
1459 Main Street
Dublin, NH 03444
603.563.7788

Bi-Glass of CT
41 Maselli
Newington, CT 06111
860.523.0703

team players

Amer Electric

Dennis Amer
Gary Hunt
Jodh Tenney
Alex Chase
Don Hackler
John Rokes

Artistic Director

Andy Macie

Bi-Glass of CT

Dick Fritzer

Boston Public Library,
Fine Arts Department

Kimberly Terry

Clough Harbour and Associates (CHA)

Marty Risley
Kevin Thatcher

Cox Woodworking, Inc.

Terry Cox
Shawn Bushway
Craig Stavseth
James Merritt

Creations in Stone / Keene Monument
Company

Corey Rice
Matt Lake
Bryan Ross
Edward Brisbois
Kevin Thompson
Tyler Towne
Daniel Tardie
Jay Blanchard

Cushing & Sons Water Well Drilling

Bart Cushing
Shawn Beal
William Monroe
Mike Sanders
Dan Winslow
Josh Byrnes
Patrick Kiniry
Jeff Cushing
Todd Arseneault
Richard Hayes

Downing Engineering

Russ Downing

Dublin, New Hampshire, History

George B. Foote, Jr.

Dublin Public Library

Elizabeth McIntyre

Froling LLC

Mark Froling
Toby Wells
George May
Isaac Lombard
Rob Plaszewski
Judy Hallquist

H3 Hardy Collaboration Architecture LLC

Hugh Hardy, FAIA
Margaret Sullivan
Mercedes Armillas

Historical Society of Cheshire County

Alan F. Rumrill

Interval Construction

Matthew Tolman
Chris Raymond, Sr
Rob McPherson
Chris Crowell
Mark Paquette
Derek Bryant
Jesse Willard

Intrepid Aerial Photography

Stephen A. Roe

Jane MacLeish Landscapes

Jane MacLeish

Kohler & Lewis

Dan Lewis

Lang Door & Hardware, Inc.

Steve Cardin

Legrand Masonry

Kris Legrand
Scott Chase
Dan Saunders
Eric Kenny

MacMillin Company, Inc.

Peter Bonneau
Mark MacKenzie
Kurt Mackenzie
Randy Black
Danny Black
Jack Wyman
Bill Greenwood
Brian Hildreth
Bob Davis
Doug Lancey

Oakridge Excavation. Inc.

J. J. Bernier

Overhead Door of Concord

Rich Sarno

Patenaude Pool Plasterers, Inc.

Andre Patenaude
Lee Patenaude
Nathan Fields
Dana Forbes
Ernest Fortin

Quality Design Nor'easter Swimming Pools, Inc.

Edward C. Payne, III
Matthew Raitt
John F. Raitt
Jose Anaya
Hector Anaya
Beto Ortega
William Seger
Ann Pyburn

S & S Painting, Inc.

Sharon Greatbach
Jana Branch
Jona Young
Kenny Young
Scott Davis
Amber Joyce
Rick Robichaud
Sherry Cook
Lisa Carey
Ronell Bell
Shane Franks
Wendy Milliken
Anne Deane
David Shelley

Scully/Architects

Daniel Scully
Katie Cassidy Sutherland
Andrew Weglinski

S.E.E.D.S. Sustainable Energy Education & Demonstration Services

Margaret Dillon

Simpson Landscape

Chuck Simpson
Justin Young
Lou Ann Poor
Allison McCabe
Amy Boyle
Steve Philbin
Ethan McBrien
Niko Prestipino
Tyler Joseph

Stebbins Spectacular Painting

Tim Stebbins

SVE Associates

Russ Huntley
Robin Freiman
Jed Pacquin
Steve Sears

The Dublin Historical Society

Nancy Campbell
John Harris
Lisa Foote

T.R. Fellows Engineering

Ted Fellows

Wilder Plumbing & Heating, Inc.

Jeff Wilder
C. Mike Anders
Mike Codman
Ben Hayes
Graham Slammin
Jay Raitto

Windmill Hill Cabinets

Jack Kurilla

Window Master
Dublin Sash Systems

David G. Voorhis
John Barbaro
Timothy Patch
Scott Hillock
Jon Hillock
Lori Scanlon
Scott McCord
Nick Lloyd
Adam Kovacs
Cory Trudelle
Tom Peterson
Ron Whitney

SPECIAL THANKS TO:

John Harris, Nancy Campbell, and Lisa Foote at the Dublin Historical Society for their tireless help in uncovering period photos of Dublin and of Stonlea itself, and for permission to use them.

Elizabeth McIntyre at the Dublin Public Library and the The Henry D. Allison Glass Negative Collection, for help in locating images of nineteenth-century Dublin and of Stonlea. And to Willard W. Goodwin, chairman of the library's Trustees, for permission to use photographs from the library collections.

Bruce Keough, president of The Dublin Lake Club, for permission to use photographs from the centennial history of the club written by Richard Meryman, Jr.

Margaret Sullivan of H3, Dan Scully and Katie Cassidy Sutherland of Scully/Architects, and Peter Bonneau of MacMillin Company, who were all extremely helpful in providing photographs and explanations of how the work was done.

Kimberly Terry at the Boston Public Library, Fine Arts Department, for giving us access to the original Peabody & Stearns drawings.

Scott Manning of Scott Manning & Associates, publicist with flair and reach.

And to the entire team at Bauhan Publishing.

PHOTO CREDITS

All images reproduced in this book are used by permission.
All photographs not otherwise credited are by Peter W. Clement and Victoria Chave Clement.

1891—First Floor Plan

1898/1903—First Floor Plan

1891—Second Floor Plan

1898/1903—Second Floor Plan

1891—Third Floor Plan

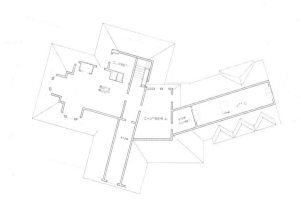

1898/1903—Third FloorPlan